INISHTOOSKERT

GREAT BLASKET ISLAND

INISHTEARAGHT
Tearaght I.

INISHNABRO

INISHVICKILLANE

THE BLASKETS — A KERRY ISLAND LIBRARY

THE BLASKETS
A KERRY ISLAND LIBRARY

by Muiris Mac Conghail

COUNTRY HOUSE

This book is supported by CRH plc

Published in 1987 by
Country House
2 Cambridge Villas
Rathmines
Dublin 6
Ireland

Country House is an imprint of Amach Faoin Aer Teo.

British Library Cataloguing in Publication Data
Mac Conghail, Muiris
The Blasket Islands.
1. Blasket Islands (Ireland) — History
1. Title
941.9'6   DA990.B65

ISBN 0-94617-212-9

Managing editor — Treasa Coady
Text editors — Siobhán Parkinson, Carina Rourke
Jacket design — Steve Averill
Book design — Bill Murphy
Typeset by Printset & Design Ltd., Dublin
Colour reproduction — Kulor Centre
Printed in Dublin by Criterion Press

To the memory of my parents
Maurice Mac Gonigal, RHA (1900-79)
Aida Mac Gonigal (1915-79)
and
to my wife Máire,
my partner in this as in all other ventures

CONTENTS

Acknowledgements 9

Preface 11

PART I
The Blasket Islands

CHAPTER 1
The Blasket Archipelago 27

Chapter 2
The Village and Islanders 37

Chapter 3
The Island Economy 43

PART II
The Blasket Library

Chapter 1
Tomás Ó Criomhthain and Outside Influence 127

Chapter 2
Muiris Ó Súilleabháin and George Thomson 148

Chapter 3
Peig Sayers 156

Genealogical Charts 164

Bibliography 168

Index 170

ACKNOWLEDGEMENTS

Muintir an Oileáin: Máire Ní Ghuithín-Cíobháin; Seán Ó Guithín; Tomás Ó Dála (Tom na hInise); Seán Pheats Taim Ó Cearna; Seán Faoillí Ó Catháin; Bríd Bean Sheáin Í Chatháin; Seáinín Mhicíl Ó Súilleabháin; Gearóid Cheaist Ó Catháin; Niamh Uí Laoithe; Pádraig Ua Maoileoin; Cáit Bean Í Mhaoilchiaráin.

Breandán and Máire Feiritéar, who shared their vast store of knowledge with me; an tAthair Mícheál Ó Cíosáin; Seosamh Ó Dála; an tAthair Pádraig Ó Fiannachta, Ollamh, Coláiste Phádraig, Má Nuad; Seán Ó Lúing; Nessa Bean Í Dheoráin; Máire Ní Ghearailt (Bean Í Bhriain), the last teacher in the Island school; Maura Lee, who found many of the photographs for me; Donncha Ó Conchúir; leanaí scoil Dhún Chaoin; sliocht an Oileáin.

Katharine Thomson; the late Professor George Thomson (Seoirse Mac Tomáis); Professor Kenneth Jackson, for his help and advice, and also for photographs by the late Thomas Waddicor; Professor Bo Almqvist, Department of Irish Folklore, University College, Dublin, for generous access to the photographs of Carl Von Sydow, George Chambers, Tomás Ó Muircheartaigh, Caoimhín Ó Danachair, Thomas Mason, and for the Robin Flower papers; Síle Flower; Patrick Flower, for many kindnesses and photographs; Veronica Zabel, for George Chambers's photographs; Professor Dr Magne Oftedal, Keltisk Institutt, University of Oslo, for the Marstrander papers; Jan Erik Redkal, Univeristy of Oslo; Mie Berg; *Verdens Gang*, Oslo; Professor Tom Biuso; Márta Ní Riada; Léan Ní Chonnalláin; Maria Simonds-Gooding; Professor Seán Ó Coileáin, University College, Cork; Professor Seán Ó Cinnéide, University College, Galway; Seán Ó Mórdha; Walter MacGrath; M.P.L. Costelloe; the late Professor E.G. Quin; Nóra Ní Shúilleabháin; Seán Ó Faoláin; Maura Scannell, for important bibliographical items; the Director, National Library of Ireland, for Ó Criomhthain mss; the Director, National Gallery of Ireland; Bridget Dolan, Royal Irish Academy, for Windele papers and an extract from the *Proceedings*; Kathleen Browne, Kerry County Library, for access to the papers of An Seabhac; Public Record Office of Ireland, for census and other material; Trinity College Dublin, for Synge papers and photographs; Director General of Radio Telefís Éireann, for photographs and archival material and for the use of material which I collected for the film on the Blaskets, *Oileán Éile — Another Island*, 1985; my friends and former colleagues in RTÉ; Betty Scannell; Siobhán Parkinson; Carina Rourke; and Treasa Coady, my publisher, who insisted that it happen.

PREFACE

Which way will I open up the Blaskets to you? By road out along the sinewy arm of the Corca Dhuibhne peninsula from the town of Tralee; then by Ventry or Ballyferriter to the harbour at Dún Chaoin to cross by ferry or, if you are very lucky, in one of the few remaining tarred-canvas boats of the area known as *naomhóga*? Or by sea, coming from the south across the bay of Dingle from Caherciveen or Valencia in Uíbh Ráthach?

Whichever way you choose, you must at the end of your journey make your way into the Blasket sound — An Bealach, a treacherous enough stretch of water it can be too. Then into Caladh an Oileáin, the small breakwater and harbour of the Great Island.

Each island that I know has its own special quality; an impression of light and sky, distance and high sea. Some travellers go into an island in search of unusual flora and fauna, or to visit remains of earlier cultures — stone forts or inscribed crosses. Some go to escape and others to find.

Our little cluster of islands, with the Great Blasket sitting in the middle, is worth visiting for all these reasons. Here you can contemplate Ireland or even turn your back to her and to the busy world for a while and gaze out towards America or up at the vast expanse of an Atlantic sky for hours. But the special attribute of the Great Blasket is the literary legacy left by its people: there is a small but important 'library' of books written by the Islanders in their native Irish. Some of these books are now available also in English, German, French, Czech and Swedish. Not all of these books are of equal merit, but taken together they represent an extraordinary collective literary achievement. How did a small island fishing community off the south-west coast of Ireland come to produce these books in a language that was hovering even then between life and death?

The best way I can open up the Islands to you is to introduce you to those books. Take an Island volume with you in your satchel and walk up through the village to Barr an Bhaile, passing by Slinneán Bán where the 'new' houses are, out along the village fields and down to An Trá Bhán (the white strand). Within that area lived eight writers, of which at least two can be reckoned as major. Just rest, contemplate the remains of the village, now vanishing into the side of the hill, and consider the sheer effort involved for a writer in such a situation. But write they did.

This book tells the story of how the village in the centre of that cluster of islands came to produce a library of books. The Island community was just on the verge of change from a traditional oral culture to a modern literate one. The community, as if they were aware that their culture was waning, began to record aspects of that culture and express themselves creatively in writing.

In this venture they were assisted by a number of visiting scholars who had come to the Island to learn Irish. The scholar visitors were sensitive to the cultural interests of the community and their encouragement was a decisive factor in both the decision to write and the choice of language. Without those visiting scholars, the Islanders might never have undertaken the task of writing, which in their circumstances on a remote island was a major undertaking. The visiting scholars added some volumes of their own to the Island library, so that it now stands at some twenty volumes.

My father was a painter and my mother a writer and they spent all their summers working in the west of Ireland. They introduced me to the culture and language of the Irish-speaking part of Ireland. At the age of eleven, while my father was painting in west Kerry, I had my first sight of the Blaskets. I didn't realise then that the final trauma of evacuation was under way. My parents gave me a copy in English translation of Muiris Ó Súilleabháin's *Twenty Years a-Growing* (*Fiche Blian ag Fás*). That book had an effect on me and still has: it rings in my ears. The original Irish version had been long out of print and it was my mother who finally bought a copy for me of the original text from the catalogue of a London bookseller.

I made a television film about the Blasket Island community which was first shown in 1985. By then the Island community had been dispersed for over thirty years, but I was fortunate enough to meet and work with many of them, and with some of the surviving scholar visitors who sustained them in their literary odyssey.

The first part of this book looks at the islands themselves: their history and the way of life and culture of the people who lived on the islands. The second part deals with the Island writers and their scholar friends.

An tOileán Tiar,
the Great Island of the Blaskets,
seen from Mám Clasach,
the gap in the hill on the road from Dingle.
The Island is like 'a great whale
surrounded by her young'.
Inis Icileáin to the left,
Inis na Bró behind the Great Island,
Tiaracht with its lighthouse and Inis Tuaisceart
to the right.

Aodan O Conchur

An tOileán Tiar,
the Great Blasket island,
with the parish of Dún Chaoin
in the foreground.
Many of the Islanders
had relatives living here
and when the Island was evacuated
the Islanders came to live here,
looking out to their old homes.

Aodán O Conchuir

The Island strand, An Trá Bhán,
a nursery for seals.
A hundred years ago
the seal was an important source of food
for the Islanders.
The oil from the seal
kept a light in every house.

Aodán O Conchúir

The Island village,
now deserted
except for the occasional use
made of some of the houses
as a fishing base.
The village is slowly vanishing
into the hill on which it was built.

The village,
looking out towards the mainland
with Cruach Mhárthain on the horizon.
The house at the top of the village
was that of
Tomás Mháire Bhell Eoghain Í Dhuinnshlé.

Aodán O Conchúir

Aodán O Conchúir

A house at Bun an Bhaile,
bottom of the village.
An Ó Duinnshlé house,
it is still used in the summer
by a member of the family.
This is the only one
of the older type of Island house
built over a hundred years ago
which is preserved.
Every house on the Island
had two rooms
and a felt and timbered roof.

Aodán Ó Conchúir

The Blasket sound,
An Bealach,
lies between Ceann an Dúna
to the left and the Great Island,
a treacherous piece of water.
A ship from the Spanish Armada
sank here in 1588.
The Islanders had to cross
from Ceann an Dúna
into the small breakwater
which was a haven for their boats,
a sea journey
of some three miles (4.8 kilometres).

Aodán Ó Conchúir

The village:
the house of Eoghan Bán,
weaver, and below it
the remains of Scoil an tSúip
the 'soupers' or Protestant school.
The Dingle
and Ventry Missionary Society
was active here in the 1840s
and the schoolteacher
lived in Eoghan's house.
There was still
a couple in the Island in 1901
who described themselves as
members of the 'Irish Church'.

Aodán O Conchúir

Aodán O Conchúir

The village:
the house of Seán Cheaist Ó Catháin
and his wife Bríd.
Seán Cheaist
was one of the Island musicians:
he played the fiddle.
It was from Seán
that I recorded the fairy music
from Inis Icíleáin,
'Caoineadh na bPúcaí'.

The village:
Bóithrín na Marbh,
the road of the dead.
It was down along this path
that the Islanders carried their dead
to the small harbour
and then by *naomhóg*,
the small tarred-canvas canoe,
across the sound
to Dún Chaoin for burial.
It was down this path that the
remains of Tomás Ó Criomhthain
were brought on a snowy day in 1937.

Aodán O Conchúir

The village strand,
An Trá Bhán.
Here the men of the village
played the game of hurling.
Tomás Ó Criomhthain
describes one such game
on a Christmas day
when the two sides drove one another
in and out of the water.
Bruised men with broken limbs
were convalescents for weeks
after the marathon game.

Aodán O Conchúir

Aodán Ó Conchúir

Looking down over the village.
To the left lies An Trá Bhán
which provided seaweed
for fertiliser in the neap tides.
The visitors to the Island
swam there and it was off the strand
that Tomás Ó Criomhthain's son
drowned in an attempt
to rescue Eveleen Nicholls,
a close friend of Patrick Pearse

Inis Tuaisceart:
the prehistoric *clochán* on the island
was lived in by a number of families
from 1830 to 1850.
The antiquary, John Windele,
met Tomás Ó Catháin's wife,
Peig, and her family there in 1838.
Some years later,
the island became stormbound
for some six weeks.

Aodán O Conchúir

Tomás died in the stone hut
and his body putrefied:
his wife, being too weak
to carry it out,
began to dismember it in the hut
and cast the pieces out.
She later went insane.

An Tiaracht:
the lighthouse and living quarters
of the lighthouse
are perched on the side
of this massive rock face.
The light has been functioning
since 1870.
The fog signal ceased to operate
in May 1987.
The Islanders used to sail under the archway,
Poll na Stiúrach,
but it could only be done
by the most skilled boatmen.

Aodán Ó Conchúir

Inis na Bró,
'quernstone island',
lies off the southernmost point
of the Great Blasket,
called the 'cathedral rocks'
by some visiting sailors
for obvious reasons.
The Inis was a very rich hunting ground
for seals and it was here
that the Islanders hunted
in and out among the rocks.

Aodán O Conchúir

THE BLASKETS
A KERRY ISLAND LIBRARY

PART I

CHAPTER 1

The Blasket Archipelago

The Great Blasket island forms part of a cluster of seven islands and several islets and rocks, which lie off the south-west coast of County Kerry, in the Barony of Corca Dhuibhne, on the north side of the entrance to Dingle Bay. Looking out at the archipelago from Slea Head on the mainland, Inis Icíleáin is to the south-west; Inis na Bró to the west; and further west, behind the Great Blasket, is Tiaracht, which has a lighthouse; to the north lies Inis Tuaisceart; and off the east of the Great Blasket are Beiginis and Oileán na nÓg. The Great Blasket — An tOileán Tiar or An Blascaod Mór — sits in the centre of the cluster of islands 'wallowing like a whale,' as Seán Ó Faoláin described it 'in the darkening sea surrounded by its twelve young'. Collectively the island group is known as the Blaskets.

Folk etymology suggests that the name 'Blasket' contains the Irish word *blaosc* meaning shell, implying a shell-like appearance for the Island. The name in various forms goes back to at least the beginning of the fourteenth century, so it obviously has a long history and must be centuries older than its first recording. It seems reasonably certain, however, that the word 'Blasket' or 'Blascaod' is not Irish in origin. Robin Flower, the well-known scholar and writer about the Island, sensed a Viking connection, and suggested that the word is derived from the Norse *brasker*, meaning a sharp reef. If that derivation is correct it is certainly an apt description for the Island when viewed from the sea.

The landscape of the Corca Dhuibhne or Dingle peninsula is dominated by a mountainy ridge, which runs the whole thirty-mile (forty-eight-kilometre) length of the peninsula from Tralee out to Sliabh an Iolair at Dún Chaoin and reappears from under the sea at the Great Blasket itself. The coastline of the mainland and of the islands is composed of steep and at times sheer cliff edges with occasional coves and inlets. The whole area was subject to great volcanic activity and the underlying geological formation is old red sandstone. An ice-mass probably moved from Conamara, came over the Smerwick Harbour area and stopped at Slea Head and the Blasket Islands.

At any event, the islands today look remarkably like the tops of a range of mountains and hills whose valleys and glens are now buried in the sea about them. To gain access to the islands you have to climb and climb, even on the Great Blasket. It is like trying to enter a building at the third floor.

The Blaskets in ancient times

It appears that the islands were inhabited from a very early time. Excavations not far away on the mainland at Cuan an Chaoil have revealed a mesolithic (middle Stone Age) settlement on the edge of the ocean well before 6000 BC. After the mesolithic hunter-gatherers came the neolithic (late Stone Age) period, when the earliest farmers learned to cultivate the soil and herd the animals instead of roving about in search of food. However, there has been no evidence for neolithic settlement in the west Kerry area as yet.

In the Iron Age the builders of the promontory forts emerged, and our first piece of evidence of human life on the Blaskets is the promontory fort at the north-west end of the Great Blasket. It is called An Dún (the fort) and it is located right on the edge of a cliff overlooking Carraig an Lóchair and a sheer cliff face to the sea. As farming gradually came to dominate the economy, ringforts, essentially well-fortified farmsteads, came to be built, and there are plenty of these in the Corca Dhuibhne area.

Inis Icíleáin

The most southerly of the Blaskets, Inis Icíleáin, has the remains of what is probably an early monastic site which contains a lintelled doorway in the east wall and a graveyard with a *leacht* or gravestone. An inscription on a stone cross here was read by the archaeologist, the late Professor R.A.S. Macalister, as OR DO MACRUED Ú DALACH, a mixture of Irish and Latin meaning 'Pray for Macrued, grandson of Dálach'. This stone is now missing. Charles J. Haughey TD, the present Taoiseach, acquired the island in recent times and has built a summer house on it.

The name 'Inis Icíleáin' is difficult to explain. The first element *inis* is clear enough: 'an island'. The second element may contain the Norse word *vik*, which means 'bay' or 'harbour', and the final element might be a personal name, so Inis Icíleáin could mean 'island harbour' or 'bay of Ileán' (a personal name) or 'bay of *faoileán*' (a seagull); on the other hand the final element may be *oileán*, another Irish word for 'island', giving us 'islandbay island'. I believe that many of the west Kerry coastal names contain Norse elements, but there is still a considerable amount of work to be done in unravelling the linguistic patchwork.

Professor Seán Ó Cinnéide draws our attention to an entry in the Annals of Inis Fallen (now preserved in the Bodleian Library, Oxford) under the year 1040, where the death of one Gilla Meic Oíbleáin Ua Conghaile, King of Corca Dhuibhne, is recorded. There was also a bishop of the same name whose death is recorded in the annals in 1166. Both king and bishop owe their name to Oíbleán, a saint in the west Kerry area in the seventh century or perhaps earlier, and it seems possible that

Inis Icíleáin might have been an island sanctuary of his cult. If that is correct then the island's earlier name would have been Inis Mhic Oíbleáin.

Inis Icíleáin is a source of much folklore, and the story of the folk air 'Caoineadh na bhFairies', 'Caoineadh na bPúcaí', 'Port na bPúcaí' or 'The Fairies' Lament' is one of the best known. This is how Tom Daly na hInise or Tomás Ó Dála, a former inhabitant of Inis Icíleáin, told the story:

Tháinig an bhean lasmuigh dhon dtigh, agus í ag amhrán, ag rá an phoirt — and t-aer, abair, an fonn aici — agus bhí duine éigin istigh acu go raibh cluas aige, bhí sé ag fhéin ar maidin, bhí an bhean bailithe lei. Bhí focail leis:

Is bean ón slua sí mé, tháinig thar toinn
Agus go goideadh san oíche mé tamall thar lear,
'S go bhfuilim sa ríocht, fé gheasa mná sí,
Agus ní bheadsa ar an saol so, ach go nglaofaidh an coileach
Caithfeadsa féin tabhairt fén lios isteach,
Ní taitneamh liom é ach caithfead tabhairt fé
Agus a bhfuil ar an saol so caithfead imeacht as.

The fairy woman came to the outside of the house and she was singing, saying the tune and there was someone inside who had an ear for music: he had the tune by morning. The woman had vanished. There were words to it:

I'm a woman from the fairy host, who came over the wave
I was carried off by night for a while over sea
I'm in their kingdom, under control of fairy women
And I shall not be in this world after the cock crows
Then will I go into the *lios* [fairy fort]
It is not a pleasure for me but there must I go,
And all in this world must I leave.

This haunting air is an essential part of the Blasket culture and has achieved an important place in Irish traditional music. In its primary form it is played on a fiddle and formed part of the Island musicians' repertoire. I recorded a version of it from the late Seán Cheaist Ó Catháin, an Island musician and son of a musician himself. It has been suggested that the air is based on the call of a seal heard at night in one of the coves at the Inis. The Island community believes, however, that the tune represents a lament for the death of one of the fairy community whose home was also on the Inis.

Séamus Heaney's poem, 'The Given Note', is about this tune:
On the most westerly Blasket
In a dry-stone hut
He got this air out of the night ...

Inis Tuaisceart

Inis Tuaisceart (north island), the most northerly island of the cluster, looks like an island which has just capsized into the sea or is about to fall over into it. When viewed from the mainland I have always thought that it resembles the figure of a great giant asleep on the surface of the sea. Tomás Ó Criomhthain, the Island author, describes the peak at the north-east of the island as a 'círín coilig', a coxcomb, and indeed at close quarters it does look like this.

Inis Tuaisceart has an early Christian site, including an oratory known as Teampall Bréanainn (Brendan's oratory). The site is surrounded by an early field system which was probably still in use until the latter part of the nineteenth century. Certainly Blasket tradition has it that Inis Tuaisceart was a great place for growing potatoes and, like Inis Icíleáin, this island was inhabited by at least one family well into the second half of the last century. The inhabitants of Inis Tuaisceart in the last century occupied a large *clochán* which formed part of the early Christian settlement. That *clochán* indeed provides us with some indication of the living conditions of a Blasket Island family in the nineteenth century.

On 14 June 1838, the Cork antiquary John Windele, in the company of others from Cork and the parish priest of Ballyferriter, John Casey, set sail from Faill Cliath at Dún Chaoin 'in the boat provided for us and occasionally with sail spread or the men pulling lustily at the oars as the wind favoured or lulled we moved over the scarcely heaving waters steering for the centre of the archipelago which lay before us'.

As the boat and its company passed the Great Blasket, Father Casey pointed out the martello tower (smitten by lightning in the '30's) and Windele records that the priest said that the Island had a population of 'about 120'. They coasted by Inis na Bró and Inis Icíleáin, which, according to Windele was a 'great breeding locality for eagles'. 'We saw,' said Windele, 'as we approached, one of these birds perched on a rock inaccessible to man.'

When the boat and its party came to Inis Tuaisceart they had great difficulty in landing and even greater difficulty in ascending the rocks onto the island. Windele's account is exactly as I found the situation when bringing a film crew onto Inis Tuaisceart a hundred and fifty years later.

The boat party found the wife and family of an islander Tomás Ó Catháin living in the *clochán*. 'Their dwelling is one of the old circular stone roofed cells,' wrote Windele, 'the roof of which is formed by over-laying flags and the family have formed a small hole in the roof to let out the smoke.' Tomás Ó Catháin was not on the island that day having gone out to Dún Chaoin, but Windele records that Ó Catháin's wife, Peig, gave them every hospitality and ordered her son to kill a rabbit or two. Windele declined this offering. Not to be thwarted in her wish to give them something, on departure she presented Windele with a live storm petrel ('guarder', as Windele calls it, for the name *guardal*), which when out of sight of the landing place he gave to one of the boatmen who had asked him for it. The *guardal* or storm petrel was a valued delicacy of the Islanders.

That Inis Tuaisceart family came to grief some years later. They were isolated during a prolonged spell of bad weather for some six weeks. The husband died and his wife, who was too weak to move him out of the *clochán*, began to dismember his body and throw the pieces out through the smoke hole in the roof of the *clochán*: the smell of the putrefied body had become too much for her. When neighbours from the Great Island finally made their way onto Inis Tuaisceart, they found the woman in a demented condition with the half-dismembered body of her husband in the *clochán* beside her. When she recovered she was able to tell the whole gruesome story and this was recorded by another archaeologist visitor to the island, George Du Noyer, in 1856. Du Noyer visited Inis Tuaisceart to draw the early Christian remains and his drawings are still to be seen in the Royal Irish Academy in Dublin.

Both Inis Tuaisceart and Inis Icíleáin provided herding and fattening for the Islanders' stock of cattle, sheep and pigs, which were transported to the small islands by *naomhóg* (canoe or coracle), a remarkable feat in itself. The movement up and down of animals from and to sea-level on Inis Icíleáin and Inis Tuaisceart was even more remarkable.

Inis na Bró

Inis na Bró (island of the quernstone) lies off the back of the Great Blasket and to its west, between Inis Icíleáin to its south and Tiaracht to the extreme west. It is possible to recognise a 'saddle' which was part of the quern. Others suggest that the island was at one stage heavily cultivated and that corn was grown, reaped and ground on the island itself, thus giving the name. This is the most inaccessible of all the islands, although people lived on it as late as the middle of the last century: like the other islands, apart from providing a living space for the Island community, it also provided fattening and summer grazing for the main island's animal stock. *Buailteachas* or 'booleying' (moving stock to summer pastures) was a feature of the Blasket economy.

Inis na Bró also has the remains of a promontory fort on its western face and the remains of what must have been a *clochán*, known as An Múchán, and evidence of cultivation.

Travelling by boat along the north face of Inis na Bró and in line with the headland known as Ceann Dubh at the end of the Great Blasket, and across An Bealach Mór (the sound) one sees an extraordinary series of pinnacles and cliffs and arches like the great arches of a cathedral. Here in the caves of the 'cathedral' the Islanders were able to provide for themselves from the rich seal population of the island cluster.

Tiaracht

Tiaracht is the most westerly of the Blasket Island cluster and 'Tiaracht' means just that — westerly. A high, precipitous pinnacle, it is perforated by a beautiful archway which can be seen through from either direction, but only at close quarters. The rock has a lighthouse, which was first brought into service in 1870. There is a climb of some two hundred steps at an inclination of sixty degrees to the horizontal before reaching the lighthouse buildings. Tiaracht has the most westerly located funicular railway (inclined railway) in Europe for the transport of supplies, built to a gauge of three feet to three inches.

The light is exhibited from the white tower on the west end of the rock above the station, which contains living accommodation, engine rooms, storerooms and communications rooms. The light can be seen from twenty-three miles (thirty-five kilometres) away but is only visible from 318° through N to 221°, and up until May 1987 the lighthouse had a fog signal which was sounded when the archipelago was beset by fog and poor visibility.

When the Port of Dublin Corporation were purchasing Tiaracht in the nineteenth century from the landlord, the Earl of Cork, they paid £200 and a further £75 to Miss Clara Hussey for her interest in the rock under the Earl of Cork. The rock was a particular source of feathers for bedding and quilts and indeed the Islandman, Tomás Ó Criomhthain, has said that the Blasket Islanders were probably the best bedded people in the area! The feather supply explains the value which the Earl of Cork and his land agent Miss Hussey put on Tiaracht.

Tiaracht was also a source for food, particularly the flesh of the puffin or *fuipín* which both the Islanders and their landlord valued. Tradition has it that the great Daniel O'Connell ('the Liberator', parliamentarian and father of Catholic emancipation) defended the Islanders in an action taken by the Earl of Cork's sublessee to protect her claim to all the birds of Tiaracht.

Travelling back towards the Great Blasket from the lighthouse on Tiaracht, we pass Inis Tuaisceart to our north, the northern face of the Great Blasket to our south and around by An Leaca Dhúch and Trá Ghearraí at the north-eastern extremity of the Great Blasket, and, travelling at an angle to the Island strand, An Trá Bhán, we pass that strand and head for Beiginis.

Beiginis

To get into Beiginis we have to sail to the back of that island and into the small sound between Oileán na nÓg and Beiginis, called Bealach Oileáin na nÓg. Cuas Fada leads into Trá a' Loinnithe, like a small fjord sheltered in the heart of the island and virtually hidden from sight. Yes, this is the place of the Vikings and their hidden longboats.

Beiginis played an important part in the life of the Blasket Island community. It contained a well-built herdsman's dwelling, a large one from the evidence of its remains, but, most importantly, the small island bore a rich grass which could support a dairy; unfortunately there was not an adequate supply of fresh water available and drinking water had to be brought in by boat. Peig Sayers, one of the Island authors, recounts that her mother told her about the last of the dairymen on the Island, a Risteard Ó Cearúl who was married to Cáit Ní Dhálaigh. Risteard had to bring in the water from the Great Blasket by boat in barrels and on one occasion his luck ran out and poor Cáit was widowed. His death is said to be commemorated in the placename Spéir an Chearúllaigh, but I have not been able to find such a placename so far.

Oileán na nÓg

The other islets and rocks were not large enough to support human inhabitants but the small island behind Beiginis, Oileán na nÓg, provided grass for newly weaned lambs.

Apart from the main islands which we have been describing, there are over a hundred rocks and small perches of land and stone around the Blasket cluster. These and the various seaways surrounding the cluster each has its own name, although these names will die or change according as those who use or used them forget them or die themselves.

The Great Blasket

An tOileán Tiar (the western island), An Blascaod or the Great Blasket is three and a quarter miles (5.2 kilometres) long and two-thirds of a mile (one kilometre) at its widest point. The village — An Baile — is located on the eastern side of the Island, tucked into the side of the hill: just below the village is Caladh an Oileáin — the Island harbour — which is in fact a small breakwater which allowed the Islanders to moor briefly before lifting their *naomhóga* up to the *stáitsí* or perches. Looking at the village from the sea the Island's white strand — An Trá Bhán — lies along the eastern face of the Island from the village, almost to the eastern point. Although the Island at its closest point to the mainland is only about three-quarters of a mile (1.2 kilometres) off Dún Mór head, it is a sea journey of three miles (five kilometres) from the harbour, An Fhaill Mhór, at Dún Chaoin to Caladh an Oileáin on the Island, and the waters in An Bealach can be quite treacherous.

Approaching the Island by sea and leaving the rock known as An Scológ to our port side and moving closer to Beiginis on our starboard we move in towards the Island: from the sea, the Island looks massive enough rising out of it with a green front, and depending on the weather and light conditions a series of humps protruding from behind the green face which can alter from purple brown to very dark green. As we move closer, you become less concerned with the massive bulk of the whole landmass but rather begin to notice, to the right of the Island, An Trá Bhán and the green fields with little zigzag enclosures outlining them, the first discernible evidence of habitation. The field system runs from left to right between the village and the extreme right-hand corner of the Island. When the boat moves closer to the Island you begin to notice the height of the cliffs and the fact that the Island itself is virtually raised on cliff-stilts way up out of the water. Like all the Blasket Islands, with the exception of Beiginis, access onto the Island land is quite difficult.

The landing place itself — Caladh an Oileáin — almost lies under the face of the Island across from the mainland. A small fjord, the 'harbour' is in fact formed by a breakwater erected by the Congested Districts Board, which was responsible for housing, roads and harbours, in 1910: before that the Island community used several landing points according as tide, weather and season allowed, always moving their boats up onto land. In the days when the Island was populated you could gauge the number of its inhabitants by the number of *naomhóga* resting on their perches above the landing place: the boats lay from the top of the slipway right up to the beginning of Bóthar Bhun an Bhaile. The old photographs taken in the 1920s and 1930s show the strength of the population.

The population of the Blasket Islands

1821	128
1835	123

(A census taken by Father Casey, the parish priest of Ballyferriter, shows that Inis Tuaisceart, Beiginis and Inis Icíleáin were occupied.)

1841	156

(of which 3 people lived on Inis Icíleáin)

1851	109

(of which 8 people lived on Inis Icíleáin and 4 people on Inis na Bró)

1861	98
1871	138
1881	148
1891	139
1901	151

(of which 6 people lived on Inis Icíleáin)

1911	160

(no occupancy of any of the smaller islands is recorded)

1916	176

(recorded by Tomás Ó Criomhthain in a letter to Robin Flower)

1925	150

From the early surveys done of the population and the census returns it is clear that at the height of its economic strength when the fishing was good, that is up to the first world war, the Island had a population of just under two hundred souls.

At the start of the second world war the population had dipped to under 100 and by 1947 there were 50 people and in 1953, when the Island was finally evacuated, there were just over 20 left.

An Bealach

The dairyman from Beiginis was not of course the only person to drown off one of the Blaskets. Island tradition preserved in oral form, in many cases protected in a placename or in the work of the Island authors, gives us a clear enough idea of the dangers which beset those working on the sea in their canvas-covered *naomhóga*, and on the foreshore and the cliffs in search of food.

The British Admiralty chart for the area [2790] and the associated Irish Coast Pilot give a good idea of the dangerous passages involved in the Blasket Sound — An Bealach: 'Indeed, in heavy gales from the westward the appearance of the sea among the islands borders on the terrific, and seamen accustomed to its navigation concur in describing it as a most dangerous locality at such times.'

The narrowest point between the Great Blasket and the mainland at Dún Chaoin is that between An Liúir, a narrow strip of rock terminating in a cone some 148 feet (50 metres) in height off Dún Mór, at the headland known as Ceann an Dúna, and An Gob or Gob an Gharráin, the nearest headland on the Great Blasket. The width is about three-quarters of a mile (1.2 kilometres). Lying off An Liúir is the rock called An Scológ (from the Norse *skalkr*), with a small channel between it and An Liúir, and off An Scológ is another rock, Stromboli, which was struck by HMS *Stromboli*, while on survey in the sound in 1858. Little damage was done.

To the west of this rock is a reef and it is upon this Stromboli reef that a ship of the Spanish Armada, the *Santa Maria de la Rosa*, came to grief on Wednesday, 21 September 1588. The *Santa Maria* was one of a fleet of about 130 ships which set sail from Lisbon in May 1588: after appalling weather and storms they re-formed at Corunna before sailing to England where they fought the English naval forces during August and were finally forced to retreat northwards to Scotland and thence to Ireland and south by the coast from Donegal to Sligo, Mayo, Galway, Clare and to the Blaskets and southwards. The *Santa Maria de la Rosa* was 945 tons and carried twenty-six guns and 297 personnel. There is some evidence to suggest that an illegitimate son of the King of Spain, the Prince d'Ascoli, was lost with the ship. We are still awaiting the detailed results of survey and excavation work carried out at the site of the disaster, particularly in the years 1968 and 1969 when the *Santa Maria* was discovered.

This was not the first appearance by Spanish ships off the Kerry coast: just five years previously a force of over 700 Spanish, Italian and Irish landed, in September 1580, at Smerwick Harbour at the promontory fort known as Dún an Óir. They had been dispatched from Santander in the previous August to support the rebellion against Queen Elizabeth led by the Earl of Desmond. Although well armed and supplied with a strong defensive position, the allied force surrendered after three days and all but a few were slaughtered by the English forces.

The poet Edmund Spenser, author of *The Faerie Queen*, was present at the siege of Dún an Óir as secretary to the commander of the English force, Lord Grey. Another distinguished Englishman, Sir Walter Raleigh, was also present and was active in the siege itself if not in fact in the execution of the invasion force. Such is the surviving tradition in the Corca Dhuibhne area that children were until quite recently disciplined by their mothers by being told: 'Chughat an Rálach!' (Raleigh is going to get you!), and indeed the phrase 'Marú an Dúna ort!' (the massacre of the Dún upon you!) is still used as a malediction.

CHAPTER 2

The Village and Islanders

The village on the Great Blasket, known simply as An Baile (the village), was quite an elaborate one. It was divided in two halves. That nearest An Caladh (the harbour) at the bottom was known as Bun an Bhaile (bottom of the village) and the top half was known as Barr an Bhaile (top of the village). The whole village lies in against the side of the hill for shelter. From the time you come into the Island virtually all movement is up and against the hill. You certainly see this when moving up through the remains of the village. The other thing about the village is the network of paths, some large enough, some small, running hither and thither, crossing one another here and there. The network shows, even now, the close ties of the members of the community with each other and the constant visiting of each other's houses.

At Bun an Bhaile you had two Ó Súilleabháin households, the one further to the left towards An Gob being one of the musical families of the Island. That house also kept some summer guests. The other Ó Súilleabháin house at this part of An Baile was the home of Muiris Ó Súilleabháin, author of *Twenty Years a-Growing*: his grandfather's house, the house of Daideo Eoghan, was above that again. There was also the house of Muintir Cheaist, as this Ó Catháin family was called, of whom Ceaist himself and his son Seán Cheaist were traditional musicians. It was from Seán Cheaist that I first heard the Inis Icíleáin fairy music 'Caoineadh na bPúcaí'. His son Gearóid, born in 1947, was the last child to be born on the Island and when he was a child enjoyed what must have been a form of paradise, for there was then no school on the Island. This was one of the reasons that the Islanders finally decided to evacuate.

The Ceaisteanna were known from their grandfather and great-grandfather as men of strength: the nickname *Ceaist* represents a tradition that one of the family had been able to lift a *ceast*, a heavy stone or lump of iron, and cast it some considerable distance. This may have occurred in Beiginis. The musical tradition is continued by the present generation of the family.

What may have been the site of a castle of the Anglo-Norman Feiritéar (known in English as Ferriter) family is at Rinn an Chaisleáin (castle point), above the Island harbour. It became a burial ground for infants and perhaps a resting place for other Islanders when the Island was stormbound or for the dead from shipwrecks.

Above Rinn an Chaisleáin is one of the few surviving traditional Island houses; this is still maintained by a member of the Ó Duinnshlé family. The houses were small and compact like the Ó Duinnshlé one. Building materials were not plentiful and many of the earlier houses were built essentially of natural unhewn stone or daub with a low-strung roof, originally perhaps of rushes or other thatch. There were one or two very small bedrooms, a kitchen and living space with an open hearth fire and a series of cupboards or a dresser. There would also have been a settle bed which doubled as a seat in the daytime and as an extra bed at night. The houses very often had a loft above the kitchen which might contain another bed, or more usually a place in which to hold supplies, fishing nets, salt, perhaps cured mackerel and other seafood, and greatcoats and oilskins if the family finances allowed of such purchases. There were two doors, one at the front and one to the back, to use in accordance with the direction of the wind and rain and two windows to the front, with perhaps a window in the loft eave of the house.

At the extremity of Bun an Bhaile lies the house of Tomás Ó Criomhthain, author of An tOileánach — the most important of the Island writers. His house, which he built himself, is built into the back of an earthen bank for protection and was small relative to some of the other houses: one bedroom behind the hearth, two kitchen windows and a bedroom window. The roof may have been originally thatched but was at a later stage of tarred canvas and wood, supported from the inside by wooden roof trusses.

At the top of the village — Barr an Bhaile — was the house of Tomás Ó Duinnshlé, and below it a house known as An Dáil (the parliament). The Islanders must have been very much in touch with events in Dublin to use the word Dáil as a term for their meeting place for debate and exchange of information. 'Dáil' was the term for the long-sought-for native legislature which came into being as a provisional parliament in 1919. The house of An Dáil — Tig na Dála — was that of Máire Ní Scannláin and it was the young people of the Island who gathered there for music and song. Below that house was the house of Maurice Mhuiris Ó Catháin and his son Seán Faoillí and a little below that was the house of Seán Mhaidhc Léan Ó Guithín, grandson of the Island 'king', Pádraig Ó Catháin. This was the house in which Robin Flower and his family stayed during their frequent visits to the Island. The Guithínigh were originally the inhabitants of Inis Icíleáin.

Below the Guithín household was the house of Pádraig Ó Catháin, known as An Rí or the King. This title of rí or 'king' was known in the social structure of some of the islands off the west coast of Ireland: Inismurray off the coast of County Sligo, Inis Gé off the Mullet peninsula in County Mayo and Tory Island off the coast of Donegal. The position of king seems to have been created by election, but the surviving evidence from the Blasket Island culture does not establish that fact clearly.

Tomás Ó Criomhthain, whose best friend was the King, Pádraig Ó Catháin, says that he had heard of another king who was of the Guithín family. He also says that Ó Catháin's grandfather, also king, had five milch cows which he had himself seen. The Guithín King, whom Tomás had only heard of through Island lore, was supposed to have had eight or ten milch cows, a mare and a wooden plough. This was considerable wealth and must have been held at the end of the eighteenth or the beginning of the nineteenth century, about 1780-1800.

The role of *rí* seems to have been one of local community leadership, particularly where a major communal effort had to be undertaken; there also appears to have been some judicial or arbitration function involved to which the community submitted. In Tomás Ó Criomhthain's time and in more recent memory the most obvious role which the *rí* enjoyed was that of postman. In time the King's son Seán took on that job, but not the kingly title: he was known as Seán an Rí (Seán [son] of the King).

School and church

Below the house of An Rí and that of his daughter, Máire Ní Ghuithín, lies the schoolhouse, roofless: gone is the echo of the youngsters' laughter. Here the Island children went to school and the traditional 'station' mass was held when the parish priest and his curate came into the Island. When the Island was at its full strength the school had two teachers. Built about 1866 the school was finally closed in 1941 on the orders of the Department of Education in Dublin: those children who were living on the Island at the time just had to be taught by their parents or sent out to school on the mainland at Dún Chaoin. The decision to close the school was one of the final blows to the community which brought about the inevitable evacuation in 1953.

Tomás Ó Criomhthain writes of his days at the school in the company of his friend the King. His first teacher was Neans Ní Dhonncha and Tomás must have gone to school for the first time a short while after the school was built. Neans left to get married and she was followed by Roibeárd Gabha, who only lasted some three months. In time Neans's sister came into the Island as teacher and she spent three years on the Island before leaving to marry as her sister had done before. Finally Tomás and An Rí were taught by an old war veteran and his crippled wife. During their term on the Island Tomás and the King acted as 'monitors', assisting or indeed standing in for the teacher, who suffered from bad health.

English was the language of the school until the last decade or so of the nineteenth century, when the educational authorities began to recognise the existence of the Irish language in the areas where it was spoken. The Islanders knew quite well that English had to be learned if they were to get ahead in the world and particularly if they were to have any chance of success in the new world of Springfield and Boston in the United States. Education in the Island school had to be a preparation for emigration: the economics of the Island community ordained it so. The problem for the teachers was put very well by the last teacher on the Island, Máire Ní Ghearailt, who wrote to me:

An obair ba chrua ar scoil ná múineadh an Bhéarla. Níor mhaith liom ligint dos na scoláirí an scoil a d'fhágaint gan eolas cuíosach maith ar an mBéarla. Thuigeas go maith cad a bhí i ndán dóibh, agus ní scéalta fiannaíochta nó rudaí mar sin ar scoil a dhéanfadh an chur chun cinn dóibh, fiú amháin munar chuadar sall go Meiriceá.

The hardest task at school was the teaching of English. I would not have wanted to let the pupils finish school without a fairly good knowledge of English. I knew quite well what was in store for them, and it was not fenian tales or the like at school which would stand to them, even if they were never to go to America.

The names on the school roll when the Island school was closed at Christmas 1941 were Máirín, Liam, Máirtín and Tomás Ó Ceárna, and Eibhlín and Máire Ní Ghuithín.

Whatever about the concern that the pupils would have enough English to survive in a world where Irish alone would have had no place, the teaching of Irish must have been of a high standard. The Islanders were literate in their own language, unusually so in the circumstances of the day. A high degree of literacy is evident in the Islanders' correspondence. Both the Island King, Pádraig Ó Catháin, and Tomás Ó Criomhthain were writing to Robin Flower in London from 1910, and the many visitors over the years maintained correspondence with the community in both Irish and English. The number of books written by the Islanders is testimony to their culture. By this stage the list stands at at least twenty volumes. Additionally there are memoirs in manuscript form, essays, published and unpublished folklore material and countless hours of radio material in the archives of Raidió na Gaeltachta (the radio service for Irish-speaking districts).

There was a time when the Island had a school for a number of Protestant families native to the Island. As late as the census taken in March 1901 the return records that there were two members of the Blasket community who described themselves as members of the 'Irish Church'. They were a husband and wife of the surname Conchúr or Connor, whose children all described themselves as Roman Catholic. The Connor family must have been the last of the Protestant community on the Island which had been in existence from about 1839. The Protestant school on the Island was built in that year and was subsequently known by the pejorative term of 'Scoil an tSúip' (the soup school). The expression 'to take the soup' meant to convert from Catholicism to Protestantism, the story being that poor Catholics were offered soup to encourage them to change their religion; like all controversies in Irish history, the word 'souperism' does an injustice, in fact, to those who were genuinely devout. The religious fervour and controversy which inhabited the Corca Dhuibhne peninsula from about 1830 was a complex one and in part represented a desire for genuine moral and social reform. There was a small but strong Protestant community in the peninsula, mostly Irish-speaking, and indeed there are still some representatives of that community living in the area to this day.

Scoil an tSúip was built in 1839 by the Reverend Charles Gayer. He had come to Dingle in 1833 as an assistant to the rector and chaplain to the local landlord, Lord Ventry. Gayer was an Englishman from Somerset and knew no Irish but he seems to have been an impressive preacher and made an impact on the population in the area. Gayer was helped in his work by Tomás Ó Muircheartaigh, a convert who was subsequently ordained for the Protestant church. Ó Muircheartaigh, being a native of the area, was able to preach and preach well. Folk memory records 'Parson M'rarity' as Tomás an Éithigh (Tomás the liar).

The school was built on land originally sold by the landlord, the Earl of Cork, to the British government to build a martello tower on the Island. The site was known as An Gort Bán (the lea-field) and is at the bottom of the village.

Perhaps the first Protestant bible-reader and teacher on the Island was John Sullivan (Eoghan Ó Súilleabháin). He was followed in time by James Jordan in 1844. Jordan is reported in 1854 as living in the school with his family. His name was still remembered on the Island in Tomás Ó Criomhthain's time, as Ó Criomhthain records that a rock from which Jordan used to fish on An Gob was known as 'stocán Jordain'.

By 1880 the schoolhouse was derelict. A botanist, Richard Barrington, who visited the Island on behalf of the Royal Irish Academy in July of that year, says that he slung his hammock from the rafters of the schoolhouse.

The religious developments in Corca Dhuibhne were not unique to that area. Intense activity occurred in almost all the Irish-speaking areas in the west of Ireland. Missionaries and missionary zeal on behalf of the reformed church, preaching and distributing the Bible in Irish were a common sight. Much of the activity centred around the Achill Missionary Settlement at Dugort, Sliabh Mór, in County Mayo, where a printing press was established to publish both the *Achill Missionary Herald and Western Witness*, and books including primers and texts in the Irish language.

One of the publications which came from the Achill centre was a reading primer which had a picture of a speckled cat on the opening page, with an Irish text describing the cat — *an cat breac* — 'the speckled cat'. The phrase provided a sobriquet for those who followed the missionary faith: the 'cat breacs' or *lucht an Chait Bhric*! It is probable that such phrases in the Irish of Corca Dhuibhne as *ar mo leabhar* (by my book, meaning the Bible) or *ar mo leabhar breac* (by my speckled book) as a form of affirmation originated in the bible-reading activity of the time.

The schoolhouse became in time a weavers' shed in which Eoghan Bán Conchúir worked. This is the same Conchúr family who opened our account on the Protestant presence on the Island. By the census of 1911, ten years later, Eoghan and his wife Cáit were dead and so was the Protestant faith on the Island.

Whatever the Protestant school and its bible-readers did for the Island, the bible-reading activity and the basic teaching of reading and writing from the primers which were distributed throughout Corca Dhuibhne must account for some of the literacy skills which the community acquired.

CHAPTER 3

The Island Economy

Life was never easy on the Blaskets. The economy was a subsistence one, the people eking out a living from the sea and the land. Nevertheless, the island cluster is a parcel of land, and as such it had a landlord as far back as the Middle Ages.

The Feiritéaraigh

The Féiritéaraigh (Ferriters), the Island chieftains, were an important Anglo-Norman family who had been in Ireland since at least the latter part of the thirteenth century. The Normans were well known for the way in which they integrated with the native population, and the Féiritéaraigh were no exception. They held lands in west Kerry, including the Blaskets, from the Earl of Desmond, and Ballyferriter is obviously named from them. They had a castle at Baile Uachtarach in Cuan an Chaoil on the mainland, and one at Rinn an Chaisleáin on the Great Blasket. Indeed, the Great Blasket was formerly known as 'Ferriter's Island'.

A scion of the Feiritéar family, Piaras Feiritéar, son of Éamann Feiritéar, was probably born in the last decade of the sixteenth century, perhaps at the family home at Cuan an Chaoil on the mainland near the present Ostán Dún an Óir or at Rinn an Chaisleáin in the Great Blasket island. Feiritéar became chieftain of his people and was also an accomplished poet in the courtly love poetry tradition (*amour courtois*).

This 'captain-poet' took the confederate side in the Cromwellian wars and forces under his control captured Tralee Castle in 1642 and he held out in Corca Dhuibhne for another ten years until defeated at Ross Castle near Killarney in 1652. Even though he had a 'parley', he was captured by the English Cromwellian forces and hanged at Cnocán na gCaorach in Killarney in 1653. Some of his work survives through the manuscript tradition. In one of his poems he treats of a Scottish poet Maol Domhnaigh Ó Muirgheasáin, who had visited all the major centres of classical or bardic poetry in the country. Feiritéar must have met the Scot; perhaps Ó Muirgheasáin made his way over to the Great Blasket? In any event the knowledge which Feiritéar displays in this poem of the state of Irish language poetry throughout the length of the country gives one an idea of his own learning and culture.

So also does his work in a more personal genre, for instance his lament for the death of Maurice FitzGerald, son of the Knight of Kerry, who had served in Philip II's army in Flanders:

Mór bhfile nár bh'fhile i gcómad	The silent versifiers must refrain,
I n-amhras ar fheabhas a n-eolais	Doubting their prowess to pursue their trade,
D'eagla ná beadh d'eagna leo san	For fear their skill but ill compass its aim,
Marbhna nach ba mharbhna cóir duit.	A verity no elegy could frame.

Máire Mhac an tSaoi's translation has rightly drawn attention to the quality of language in Feiritéar's work, which may be concealed in casual reading because of the 'disconcertingly lovable and picturesque personality' which emerges from his love poetry in the *amour courtois* tradition. Mhac an tSaoi states that the substance of our poem is 'convolute and floreate' but 'the language is limpid, natural, and full of grace ... '

The Blasket Island folklore abounds with references to Feiritéar, even to the point of identifying places on the Island where Feiritéar committed acts of valour or outwitted the English. For instance a placename at the northern face of the Island looking out towards Inis Tuasiceart is known as Scairt Phiarais — Piaras's Cave. This 'cave' was a hiding place for Piaras when pursued by the English. In Tomás Ó Criomhthain's account of the story, Piaras picked a cave in a cliff that was the sheerest and most dangerous on the Island coastline. Indeed, says Tomás, many in the Island could not even walk where the cave is. Often lonely, Piaras could hear and see the very waves leap up almost as high as the mouth of the cave. Piaras could never understand why there was a constant drip from the flagstone which forms the cave in a hideout which otherwise was as dry as a fox's den. Piaras said:

A Dhia atá thuas, an trua leat mise mar táim?	O God up there, don't you pity me as I am?
Am chaonaí uaigneach nach mór go bhfeiceam an lá	Cold, lonely, I hardly can see daylight
An braon atá thuas in uachtar lice go hard	The drip which is high up above in the flagstone
Ag titim im chluais agus fuaim na toinne lem sháil.	Falling about my ear with the sound of the wave at my feet.

From the arrival of the Anglo-Normans into the peninsula of Corca Dhuibhne and the granting of the Blaskets by the Earl of Desmond to the Feiritéar family, however associated with the Irish culture and the Irish cause that family was, the Islanders became tenants of the Island and were to remain so almost to their dispersal. Following the Desmond rebellion and the Cromwellian settlement, the Islanders, like other communities, had to provide not only a rent which was always beyond their capacity, but also to suffer at the hands of remote and at times tyrannical landowners and their agents.

If it was difficult for the Islanders to pay the rent, it was also difficult for the landlords and their agents to collect: being on an island had some advantages. There are or were many memories within the Island tradition of attempts by the landlords, supported by the constabulary, to collect the rents, some successful, others not. On one such occasion one of the last seine boats was confiscated and brought to Dingle, where it rotted on the quayside.

Tomás Ó Criomhthain describes one incident in particular where an armed frigate arrived off the Island with a force of constables and revenue men to collect the rent. As soon as the first of the boats arrived at Caladh an Oileáin and an officer stepped ashore, the women of the Island, who had assembled on the cliff above the Island landing place, threw a shower of stones down on those in the boat, forcing them to retreat. The officer, when struck, aimed his gun at one of the women:

Thug sé súilfhéachaint in airde agus chocáil an gunna díreach orthu, ach níor chorraigh aon bhean amháin ach rang déanta acu ar bharr an chalaidh ... Níor rófhada gur lig bean eile cloch síos, agus bean, agus bean, nó gur bhaineadar fothram agus macalla as an gcladach ...

Then he [the officer] glanced up and cocked the gun directly at them, but not a woman moved having formed a line above the landing place ... It was not long before another woman threw down a stone, and another woman, and another woman so that they generated a noisy echo ...

The rent collectors had to retreat in their boats and regroup. Now they tried once again to effect a landing and so agitated was one of the women with rage that she threatened to throw her child which she was nursing at the invaders when she had run out of stones. The day was with the Islanders and the rent went uncollected.

The picture which Tomás Ó Criomhthain draws of the Island women here, as in other parts of his autobiography, is evidence of the role which they played in the life of the Island and a confirmation of their burden-sharing which was to last even to the dying days of the community.

These confrontations with the landlord and his agents were quite a regular part of the community's experience and distinguished them from their relatives and friends on the adjacent mainland, although they too had to suffer at the hands of the landlord's agents up to the end of the last century. Our botanical researcher, Richard Barrington, who visited the Island on behalf of the Royal Irish Academy in June 1879 and July 1880, and who slept in his hammock in the deserted Protestant school, gives us independent confirmation of the events described by Tomás Ó Croimhthain. When Barrington arrived at Dingle

... the police informed me that an unsuccessful attempt had recently been made to serve processes on the Blasket Islanders, and that they were hostile to strangers. This proved to be correct, and I found considerable difficulty in landing. At Dunquin, a small village on the mainland, opposite the Great Blasket, the boatmen declined to row me across. I heard subsequently they suspected I was a policeman in plain clothes. All sorts of excuses were made. Finally, after four days' waiting, I procured a boat, the Rev. Father Egan, P.P., having spoken to the people on my behalf.

On approaching the Great Blasket, which is one mile distant from the nearest point of the mainland, the people were seen to run from the houses, and congregate on the edge of the cliff over the landing-place, shouting and gesticulating at the same time. Heaps of stones were piled, and the natives began to throw them at our boat.

Eventually Barrington was allowed to land and he found the community, once they realised the purpose of his visit, to be friendly and interested in his work. On his second visit, the following year, he says 'The curiosity of the natives was intense, and I suffered from intruders [in the deserted schoolhouse] when examining specimens, and placing them between the blotting sheets.'

Land and sea: the village larder

The village larder consisted of two parts: that which lay in the fields to the east of the village between it and Trá Ghearraí, and that which lay under the waves to be harvested by the Islanders from their *naomhóga*, their tarred, canvas-covered light boats. Depending on which part of An Baile the Islander lived in — Barr an Bhaile or Bun an Bhaile — the field systems could be approached from the top of the village out by the 'new ' houses on Bóthar Bharr an Bhaile or out by Tomás Ó Criomhthain's house along Bóthar Bhun an Bhaile.

In 1907 the Congested Districts Board bought the Blaskets from the estates of the Earl of Cork. This purchase allowed the board to begin to introduce certain improvements into the life of the Island, of which the continuation of work on the breakwater pier was one, the making of a road from the village to the south of the Island another, and a third was the construction of five new houses at the top of the village at An Slinneán Bán in the years 1909-11. This development gave Peig Sayers and her husband a new and badly needed home. These houses were really the last to be built on the Island and are in marked contrast to the rather spartan dwellings of the two parts (upper and lower) of the original village.

The village fields were completely reorganised after the Congested Districts Board purchased the Island and the medieval and early modern scattered system was replaced by a more consolidated system in which an Islander's holdings were on the whole situated near one another: it was quite difficult to break with the old system of rundale altogether. Each field has its own name. From the sea the field system looks like a patchwork quilt with the little road or path network as seams in the cloth.

In *Dinnsheanchas na mBlascaodaí* (placename lore of the Blaskets) (1935) Tomás Ó Criomhthain recorded some of the field names as they were known in his time:

An treasán — the cross field
Cúil an chamaraigh — camphor corner
An gort fada — the long field
Tobar an phúca — pooka's well
Ceann an ghoirt — top of the field
An ghainimh — the sandy field
Port an eidhneáin — ivy-bank
An fearann gearra — the short field
Gort an aird — field of the rise
An fhothrach — the ruin field
An gort nua — the new field
An seana ghort — the old field
Garraí gála — windy field
Béal na trá — strand's edge field
An duimhe bhocht — the poor dune field
An duimhe mhór — the great dune field
Idir-dhá-chasán — field between two paths
An treasnaigh — the transverse field

It was from these fields that the Islanders harvested potatoes, cabbage, turnips, parsnips, corn and wheat and the hay to provide for their animals in the winter. There is evidence that flax was grown in the last century and laid out to bleach on the fields.

While the Island tillage and the associated cropping activity was concentrated around the village on the eastern face of the Island, certain placenames on the south and west of the Island are an indication that cultivation if not habitation occurred there also, but that must have been over two hundred years ago. In more recent times the Islanders cut turf, which was not very good, at the back of the Island, and collected furze and scraw for their fires. In the end the turf supply was virtually dug out and the community would, like other island people, have had to bring in their fuel supply by boat from the mainland. Of course bottled gas would have been a godsend to the community but by the time that became available the last fires on the Island had been extinguished.

The Islanders also had cattle, sheep, pigs and of course domestic fowl such as hens, duck and geese. Time was when the domestic animals and the cattle were accommodated within the Islanders' houses during the course of the long and stormy and mist-shrouded winters. This practice was usual in the Ireland of the nineteenth century.

Although Tomás Ó Criomhthain recalls that one of the leading families of the Island had plough horses some time in the early part of the last century, the donkey was the essential means of transport in recent memory within the Island: turf was brought from the back of the Island on heavily loaded animals with creels.

Whatever turf was available was saved at the back of the Island at Sliabh Bharra an Dá Ghleann, which provided a kind of black hard sod used for heating in the winter, or *stuaicín* from Buaile Nua near the site of the old martello tower, now in ruins having been struck by lightning in the 1930s. A trip back to cut turf was a day's work in itself and many of the Islanders often carried the turf to their homes on their own backs.

Turf-cutting also provided an opportunity for the young men and women of the Island to meet one another in less claustrophobic surroundings: the Islanders 'courted' at the back of the Island. The collection of water by bucket was another important social activity, which gave the villagers an opportunity of conversation and the exchange of important news and information, including of course the exchange of gossip. The most important of these wells was Tobar an Phoncáin which was close by An Dáil. Here the village community met many times daily in a kind of 'stock-exchange', where information was bartered. From this vantage point Tomás Ó Criomhthain in particular observed the daily life of the Island and wrote of it in the second of his Island books *Allagar na hInise* (*Island Cross-Talk*) (1928).

Bainim amach an tobar — munar raibh mná ina stad ann ní lá go maidin é. Bhí buicéad is fiche ann, agus ní cheal uisce a choimeád ann iad ach ag ciorrú an lae ag salmaireacht lena chéile ... Bhí triúr fear ann a mbeadh a soitheach lán d'uisce faid a bhíodar ag éisteacht le salmaireacht na mban seo agus is agamsa féin a bheadh an t-ualach móna go rábach socair faid a bhíos ina measc.

I get to the well — there were women in a queue unless I'm greatly mistaken. There were one and twenty buckets and it wasn't the scarcity of water which kept them there but rather passing the day by prattling to each other ... There were three men present whose buckets would have been brimful while listening to the prattling of these women and I myself would have well and firmly clamped my turf while amongst them.

One of the most difficult tasks which faced the Islanders was the movement in and out of stock from the Island to the mainland. The animals had to be carried in and out in the *naomhóga*, the frail island canoes. 'Bhí ana-mharú ansan — that was really murder,' said Tom Dála na hInise:

O, bhíodh ana-job air, chaithfí an bhó a thabhairt síos ar an slip, agus mórán féar a bheith caite anuas agus í a leagadh ansan, agus í a cheangal, agus ana-job ar í a chuir isteach sa naomhóg, ró-throm ach bhíodh naomhóg eile ansan in éineacht le naomhóg na bó ar eagla go dtitfeadh aon ní amach ar naomhóg na bó ... bhí ana-mharú ansan.

Oh, it was an awful job, the cow would have to be taken down onto the slip, plenty of hay thrown down, lay her down, tie her, a terrible job to put her in the *naomhóg*, a burden, but another *naomhóg* would be alongside the *naomhóg* with the cow in case of anything happening to the *naomhóg* carrying the cow ... it was really murder.

Not only had the animals to be loaded but unloaded at the other end, and as we have seen in relation to the landscape here of these islands and on the adjacent mainland all movement onto land, without exception, had to be up steep inclines if not cliff edges.

The Islanders used all of the other islands, with the exception of Tiaracht, to provide summer grazing and fattening for their animals. The entry onto Inis Tuaisceart is amazing. I watched and followed Seán Pheats Taim Ó Cearna, then no longer a young man, climb the cliff face as if he were a young goat. You get to know how to balance yourself and use your back to carry weight. Taim described in some detail how he often brought sheep on and off that island by carrying them up and down the cliff face. Having selected the stock from the herd they brought them to the top of the cliff at Leac na Muice, having first shorn them, a day's work in itself, and then tying the horns of the sheep with a special knot, they would pull and jump with the sheep down the cliff edge, almost becoming in the act sheep themselves, until they got to the flagstone at the bottom. Then the problem was to tie the sheep by their feet and get them into the *naomhóga* which were bobbing and dipping up and down in the often turbulent sea: the jump was a tricky one.

Then a long row home with a heavy boat with up to fifteen sheep tied together, and the trip perhaps into Beiginis where the sheep would spend a further period feeding off the rather rich grass in that island which was reputed to have the best grass in the islands because of its saline content. Then back into the Blasket and home without having eaten anything all day. Haul the *naomhóg* up on the slip and lift it up to the *stáitsí*. Carry the heavy pack of Inis Tuaisceart wool up to their houses:

Deirimse leat ná bíodh aon teaspach orainn nuair a théimíst abhaile, gan puinn ite leis againn, ach blúire aráin, sin uile, mara mbeadh aon bhraon uisce ar an lic a dh'ólfaimíst, sin é mar a bhíomar ag obair ach go deimhin bhí caoire breátha inti, úmraí brea olann ... chuirfeá malairt éadaig ort féin, agus nuair a bheadh an tae ólta agat, dheargófá do phíp, tás ag Dia bheifeá chomh sásta le diúc ansan, bhuailfeá amach ag bothántaíocht duit féin ... bhímíst ag eachtraí dóibh mar gheall ar an lá agus cad é an marú a fuaireamar, sin é mar a chaithimís an aimsir. Bhímís chomh sásta.

I tell you, none of us would be boisterous when we went home, we'd eaten nothing, except a piece of bread, that's all, unless we had drunk a drop of water from the flagstone [in Inis Tuaisceart] that's how we worked, certainly there were fine sheep there, fine fleece ... you'd change your clothes, and when you'd had your tea, light the pipe, God knows you'd be as happy as a duke then. You'd go out visiting ... we'd tell about the day and how murderous it was, that's how we'd spend the time. We were so content.

None of Seán Pheats Taim Ó Cearna's narrative account was said with any sense of flamboyance: it was just a simple recital of everyday fact so far as he was concerned.

It was mainly from the sea, of course, that the Islanders eked out their livelihood and fed themselves. The sea-harvest was that most marketable in Dingle and to the foreign fish merchants from France, particularly Brittany, the Isle of Man and Spain. Fishing was a man's occupation; the women stayed at home and waited anxiously for their menfolk to return: some did not. Up to perhaps the middle of the nineteenth century fishing was done from large wooden fishing boats, known as 'seine' boats, requiring a large crew. These boats were replaced or superseded by the small *naomhóg* in the last century, which are canvas-covered and tarred and capable of carrying a small sail. These boats were at one stage covered by animal skin and their origin may go back to the earliest peoples on the Island and on the peninsula itself.

The word *currach* is used in other parts of the west of Ireland to indicate this coracle-type boat. The name *naomhóg* is certainly as old as the seventeenth century, where it appears in Seathrún Céitinn's history of Ireland, *Foras Feasa ar Éirinn* — 'idir loing, báirc, curachán & naomhóig' and it seems to contain the word *nae* (earlier *nó*, meaning ship or boat). Curiously there is a small cove just across from the Great Island in Cloichear called Cuas na Nae (boat cove) and our word probably means little boat or coracle. There was a tradition that the first *naomhóg* came from County Clare and that a family called Hartney from the Machairí to the north of Mount Brandon were the first builders of the boat some time in the early part of the nineteenth century. The name itself is too long established for that to be true and what we probably have in that tradition is the demise of the larger seine boat and the re-emergence of the *naomhóg*. That tradition of *naomhóg* building is still carried on in the Machairí by the Goodwyn family. I saw *naomhóga* being built at Baile na nGall in the early 1960s and more recently in Baile an Mhúraig to the north of Smerwick Harbour.

There is no doubt that these *naomhóga* were also built on the Island itself from early times and that the Islanders' prowess both in building and in handling them was well known. The typical *naomhóg* is some twenty-six feet (nine metres) in length and four and a half feet (one and a half metres) wide. The prow and the stern rise high above the water and the stern narrows considerably. There are four seats, the one in the prow capable of holding a small mast for a sail. The frame of the boat contains an intricate lattice-type interweaving, over which the canvas cover is fitted. The oars hardly have any blades and the boat moves through the water easily, gracefully and with speed. Lobster and crayfish were the most lucrative of the sea-harvest, but the Island fishermen fished for all the white fish — mackerel, whiting, pollock, herring, eel, bass. Fishing took a downward spin just at the period of the first world war, and the Islanders were not equipped to fish as far out to sea as their competitors, the French and the Manx. Their near-subsistence economy did not allow the kind of capital investment necessary to survive the changing times. But work hard on the sea they did, both out of necessity and because they enjoyed the sea, even in the face of disaster and death at times.

The long hours at sea, often with nothing to eat and nothing in their nets, gave them plenty of time to talk to one another:

Bhímíst ag caint ar gach aon ní, deirimís gur brea an lá é. 'Gúntais Dé,' adeireadh Séamas Mhéiní, 'féach an bhfuil d'éanlaithe dearga ann.' Deireadh Seán Philí ansan go raibh seoinseáil air nuair a bhídis ag eiteallaigh ró-mhór, ní chífeá Inis Icíleáin chuige an uair sin acu, ag éanlaithe dearga, lán go barra. Thabharfá leat i bpaca inniu a bhfuil innti acu. Deireadh fear eile ansan go raibh sé ina lag trá, go raibh sé in am dul ag tarrac, fear eile á rá ansan go raibh sé ina ghála gaoithe anoir is aneas, fear eile ansan, sin é mar bhímíst ag cur na slí dúinn, agus ag dul ós cionn na taoide, deireadh fear eile ansan, beidh cothrom soir againn. Deireadh fear eile ansan go dócha nach aon mhaith an seol a chur uirthi, tá sé ró dhocht, ná beadh aon chóir againn, sin é mar bhímíst ag clataráil linn, rámhaíocht mhór fhada aniar ó Inis na Bró, fanta suas go dtí'n haon déag a chlog istoíche ...

We'd talk of everything, we'd say it was a great day. 'Christsake,' says Séamas Mheiní, 'look at the number of puffins.' Seán Philí would say then that there was a change due when they [the puffins] were flying in excessive numbers, you could not see Inis Icíleáin at all because of the puffins, all over the place. You'd take what's there today in a bag. Then another would say that it was ebbing, that it was time to commence pulling in, and another man, that's the way we'd spend the time, going over the waves, then another would say that we would have a smooth passage home, another would say that it seemed that there would be little point in putting up her sail, the wind was too stiff, that we would not have a fair breeze, that's how we were as we clattered along, a long row from the west from Inis na Bró, up till eleven o'clock in the night ...

That is an account from Seán Faoillí Ó Catháin who spent his life on the sea. He used the expression when talking about the fishermen who had died and whom he had known — 'Is dócha go bhfuil siad ina mbeathaig fós ag iascach ansan, agus ná cíonn tú iad, sin é agat é — I suppose they're still alive fishing out there but you don't see them, there you have it.'

The fishing grounds were the waters surrounding the cluster of islands, and the smaller islands were often used as fishing bases or for overnight accommodation when necessary. The coastal names of the Great Island itself indicate the degree to which the Islanders travelled by its cliff faces and observed every nook and cranny on it.

When the *naomhóga* moved out from Caladh an Oileáin, they went south past An Gob and towards Inis Icíleáin. The following names are like an inventory on the southern face of the Great Island:

Screallach an ghoba — scree of the gob
Fochais an Bhrannda — a submerged rock called 'Brannda'
Cuas an scannaill — shameful creek
Scairbh na bportán — crab reef
Claointín — slight slope
Cuas na bpréachán — crow cove
An cuas dubh — the dark cove
Ceann cnuic — hill head
Na colaithe — the ledges
Cuas na mballán — great rock cove
Cuas an tseoil bháin — cove of the white sail
Cúileán an uisce — water nook (a well nearby)
Rinn na gcrothóg — skaldcrow cove
An gleann briste — the fractured cleft
An chró dhubh — the black hollow
An bheannaigh — the peak
Gleann na péiste — serpent's glen
Rinn charraig an airgid — silver rock point
Cuas an fhionna-ghlais — bright-stream cove
Cladach na bhfiach mara — cormorant rock
Fothair an gcapall — horse slope
Oileán na searrach — foal's island
Cuas na Ceannainne — cove of Ceannann (a magic cow)
Béal ae(?) múire(?) — perhaps the word for boat, *nae*?
An bas — the palm (refers to a rock)
Béal chapaill — horse mouth
Ceann dubh — black head — the furthest point at the back
of the Island, facing Inis na Bró

This is only a selection of the names from the south-west side of An tOileán Tiar. The north face is equally rich in names as are the shorelines of the other islands in the cluster. Many of the names are very old, others bestowed by the fishermen in more recent times as events, disasters or other developments or changes occurred. They represent various bench marks in the history, both social and economic, of the community. These names will die, some are already gone, as the Islanders themselves cease to use the sea and their boats and when the Islanders die, who else will follow and hear the names being called out from the boats or discuss them and their history at night on the sea?

The Islanders' diet was augmented by rabbit, seafowl and, up to the first world war, by seal, which provided not only meat but also oil to feed the Island lamps. Many of the Islanders' accounts of hunting in the last century tell of hunting seals, often at great peril to the hunters.

Sometimes the Island economy benefited from the occasional shipwrecks, when ships hit the rocks or promontories of the Island itself: shades of the Armada! Timber, copper, brass, oil and the first boxes of tea came into the Island in this way. At first the tea was thought to be a form of dye and was used to colour the homespun from the weaver's loft! However it didn't take long for it to become the essential item on the kitchen table. This came about well into the last century. Buttermilk, a drink called *sleadaí* made from seaweed, and fresh milk with potatoes were the commonplace foods. As the Island did not have a public house and there does not seem to have been a tradition of illicit distilling (given the size of the rootcrop this was not unexpected), thirsty Islanders had to make it to Dingle for whiskey or a pint: that was rare, for drink cost money and there was little of that on the Island.

Marriage and the family

The family structure on the Island was an 'extended' one, probably comprising three generations and certainly living under one roof up until the middle of the last century. When Peig Sayers was married into the Island to a member of the Ó Guithín family on 13 February 1892, she was met in her new home on the Island by her father-in-law, Seana-Michí Ó Guithín (Flint) and her mother-in-law, Máire Ní Shúilleabháin. Peig thought of her father-in-law as 'lúbaire righin láidir ab'ea é, ach bhí an t-aos á' leagadh síos — he had been a strong, well-set, agile man but age was bending him down'.

Peig was one month short of her nineteenth birthday when she married. Ten years later the records show that her father-in-law was still head of the household and her mother-in-law, a brother- and a sister-in-law, her husband Pádraig (Peatsaí Flint) and their three children were the occupants of the house.

In the census of 2 April 1911, Peig is recorded as being forty years of age and her husband Pádraig forty-nine: his parents had died in the meantime, but Peig had had ten children born alive of which six were still living.

It was not unusual for young women like Peig to have married just short of nineteen years, nor indeed was the number of children which she bore. She spent the first twenty years of her married life living at the bottom of the village in a two-roomed house which she shared with at least nine other people. In common with her neighbours, she lived in hardship on the Island: that she survived to tell her account of that tough life is a tribute to her tenacity and her will to hold on to life.

Peig was one of a number of people from the mainland who married into the Island. As she tells us in her autobiography, her people had originally come from Ventry, a parish to the east of Dún Chaoin. Others who married into the Island came from the parish of Ballyferriter, which stretches from the Island itself right up to the slopes of Mount Brandon at the north and is divided from Dingle on the east by a low ridge of hills. The sea bounds the parish on its western side.

The parish is a well-formed unit and even today it is from within its borders that marriage partners are chosen. Accordingly there was a considerable degree of blood relationships throughout the parish. One of the problems facing those who wished to marry was the availability of partners not too closely related. The Catholic church regulations on marriage and blood relationships were that it did not normally allow for marriages between people descended from a common great-great-grandparent. The church would not easily relax the rule on first cousins marrying but did provide a dispensation for marriages between second and third cousins upon the approval of the local parish priest and the consent of the bishop.

In the mainland part of the parish of Ballyferriter the choice of marriage partners was wider than that available to the Blasket Islanders. Peig herself was married into the extended family of Ó Guithín and Ó Súilleabháin from which stems almost all of the second generation of Island writers. Peig Sayers's son, Mícheál Ó Gaoithín, a poet and her biographer, was a second cousin of Muiris Ó Súilleabháin, author of *Fiche Blian ag Fás* (*Twenty Years a-Growing*) who in turn was a second cousin of Lís Ní Shúilleabháin, author of *Letters from the Great Blasket*. Lís Ní Shúilleabháin, whose paternal grandmother was Máire, a sister of Tomás Ó Criomhthain, was married to Seán Ó Criomhthain, Tomás's youngest son and author of *Lá dár Saol* (a day of our life).

There was a considerable amount of intermarriage between closely related cousins to a point which became critical when the Island was beset with its final tide of emigration and the community collapsed and disintegrated. The Islanders must have been concerned about the situation. Tomás Ó Criomhthain wrote down from island-lore a poem dealing with the situation in which a husband and wife, living presumably in America, found out that they were brother and sister. There they had met, the sister being the last of the family to arrive and not recognising her brother who had left the home perhaps just after she had been born. Tomás entitled the poem 'An Bheirt Chroí-Chráitreacht' ('The Broken-hearted Pair') and wrote a brief introduction:

Deartháir agus deirfiúr iad so do bhuail lena chéile, san tíortha thar lear, agus do phós a chéile gan fhios acu. Ach ar shroichint an chuntais dóibh — seo síos na ranna dubh-bhróin do bhí eatarthu.

This was a brother and sister who met one another abroad and they married without knowing. But when they were informed — below are the sad verses between them.

Tomás says at the end of the poem 'Very frequently these events occurred formerly and now and then yet.'

In the Island marriage was an event that followed in the natural order of things. In sheer economic terms it was necessary for the young of the household to move out and establish their own homesteads. In many cases the last to marry in a household were those caring for elderly parents; this was a difficult situation for anyone marrying into the household.

Like many an island community off the west coast of Ireland, marriage brought new ties and relationships, mostly of an economic kind relating to the small amount of land available and to the crewing of the *naomhóga* for fishing. The dowry, until recently a regular feature of Irish rural marriages, was an element in the Blasket marriage, but there is no clear evidence as to how this was arranged. Because of the collapse of the fishing industry after the end of the first world war, the Island economy did not allow for this as the major element in the marriage arrangement.

In the middle of the last century marriages were contracted by young people in their teens, but by the beginning of this century the marriage age was about eighteen to twenty years of age. In most cases marriages were arranged with the consent of the parents of both spouses, and there is evidence to suggest that in Tomás Ó Criomhthain's time marriages were made by arrangement between parents and not on the initiative of the spouses.

Children were seen as evidence of a successful marriage, and child quickly followed child. Infant mortality was high both at birth and in the early years of life. There was neither doctor nor nurse on the Island and although there were women on the Island who were skilled in such matters, many a young mother or child was lost at birth.

The Island was a small, interrelated community, and the problem was to find suitable partners from within the Island in the first instance whose blood relationship was not too close. In some cases partners were secured from the mainland or Islanders married out to the mainland, but there was always a danger that because of its isolation the Island community might intermarry too closely within itself. The Blaskets did not provide from within its shores the 'rites of passage': it housed neither church nor priest. The young were baptised and married at Ballyferriter and eventually buried on the mainland at Dún Chaoin.

THE *B*LASKETS
A KERRY ISLAND LIBRARY

One of the most difficult tasks
which faced the Islanders
was the transport of cattle
in and out of the Island.
'Bhí ana-mharú ansan'
it was really murderous,
as one of them told me.
The cow had to be laid out
on the slip and tied
before being placed
into one of the frail canvas covered *naomhóga*

George Chambers

The village boats,
naomhóga, resting on their *stáitsí*
above the breakwater
and the slip.
Eight of the boats are visible here.
There were the same number again
at the next elbow
up on the *inneoin*
and another three or four
above that again,
apart from those boats
which were on the sea
or out at Dún Chaoin.
Every boat had a crew of three or four
of the Island men.

Thomas Mason

At the back of the Island:
Sliabh Bharra an Dá Ghleann
and Barra an Dá Ghleann
were the source of the Island's turf
until it ran out in the 1930s.
Both the men
and the women of the village
came with their donkeys and creels
to collect the turf when dry:
in the end
the lack of fuel
became one of the critical points
which influenced the decision
to leave.
The tower on the top of the hill
was built during the Napoleonic period:
it was destroyed by lightning in 1934.
The figure to the left
is probably Robin Flower.

George Chambers

Boat-building on the Island:
the frame of a *naomhóg*
to be covered
by a tarred-canvas skin.
The origin of the *naomhóg*
goes back a long way.
There is no doubt that boats
were originally covered
with animal skins:
tanned hide of cow or bullock
and perhaps sealskin.
The Blasket Islanders
were skilled craftsmen.

The post comes into the Island harbour.
Seán an Rí,
the King's son, was the postman
when this photograph was taken.
The *naomhóg* with the post
has just come in from Dún Chaoin.

Happy beachcombers!
A well-encrusted piece of sea wreck
served as both fuel
and timber for carving
to occupy the long winter months.
An Trá Bhán,
the white strand of the village,
was an important part
of the Island economy.
Dún Chaoin is in the background
across the sound.

George Chambers

A load of sand from An Trá Bhán.
The Islanders spread clean sand
from the white strand
on their kitchen floors.
Muiris Ó Súilleabháin,
when he came home for the first time,
saw the dry sand sparkling
on the floor in the lamplight'.
Here one of the Island girls
fetches a sack of sand
on the donkey
along one of the paths up from
the strand between the Island's fields:
it is early evening.

George Chambers

Sheep-shearing on the Blaskets.
The sheep were sheared
on Trá Ghearraí
and the wool was brought
to Dún Chaoin for
carding or for sale
in Dingle.
The Island had one weaver,
but many of the women
of the Island made homespun
for clothing.

George Chambers

An Baile, the village,
tucked in against the hill
on a cold morning.
To the right
is Rinn an Chaisleáin
(castle point),
the site of Piaras Feiritéar's
stronghold on the Island,
and it was used by the Islanders
as a graveyard for infants,
or when stormbound
when the dead
could not be brought out
to the mainland for burial.

George Chambers

Caladh an Oileáin,
the Island harbour,
at low tide.
High above the little harbour
children watch the coming
of the latest visitor
to the Island
in the post boat.

Thomas Mason

The Island scholars:
an outdoor class.
The greatest task
facing their teacher
was to prepare the children
for the long road to America.
English was an essential subject.

The Island school,
Scoil an Bhlascaoid, 1931:
one long room
with two windows at the back
and three to the front.
A felt-tarred roof
covered the school.
In the winter
a fire was fuelled by the pupils
from their own daily turf supply.
Beside the great map of Ireland
on the wall inside,
there was a picture
of an apple tree
with apples growing on it:
as the children had never seen a tree,
this was a matter of great interest.
The schoolteacher
was Nóra Ní Shéaghdha
from Paróiste Chill Chúáin
to the north of the parish.
Nóra Ní Shéaghdha was a writer
and published two novels in Irish.

Thomas Mason

George Chambers

A lobster boat:
a slightly smaller *naomhóg*
used by one of the Islanders
(Mistéal) to fish for lobster.
The cane for the pots
was cut at Baile an Ghoilín
near Dingle.
This *naomhóg*
is unusual in its design:
notice the cut
at the gunwale
for handling pots on the sea
and another at the stern
of the boat for the same purpose.

George Chambers

George Chambers

Inis Icíleáin:
the landing place at the Inis,
An Rinn Chaol.
As on all the islands
of the Blasket cluster,
a cliff climb
awaits both inhabitants and visitors.
The Ó Dála brothers
have just come ashore
from the Great Island.

Inis Icíleáin:
the house on the Inis
where the Ó Dála family lived.
Here at Log na bhFiolar
(eagle place) people from the Great Island
often visited
the Ó Dála family at their home,
Tig na hInise.
The southern face
of the Great Blasket
and the mainland at Dún Chaoin
is in view from Tig na hInise.

George Chambers

Marta Ní Riada

Tomás Ó Dála (Tom na hInise)
and a model boat under sail.
The Ó Dála family
were skilled craftsmen.
This boat was made
from salvaged wreck wood.

Inis Icíleáin:
Tomás and Pádraig Ó Dála
(Dálaigh na hInise)
outside their old home
Tig na hInise
at Log na bhFiolar.
Although the Ó Dála family
had moved into the Great Blasket
by 1911, they maintained
a presence on the Inis
with their sheep
and they fished off the Inis.
It was outside this house
that a *beansí*,
a fairywoman,
was heard to sing
'Caoineadh na bPúcaí'.

Maria Simonds-Gooding

Tig na hInise
at Log na bhFiolar,
Inis Icíleáin.
A visit by Eibhlís Ní Shúilleabháin
in 1931.
Left to right:
Tomás (na hInise) Ó Dála, Eibhlís Ní Shúilleabháin,
Nóra Ní Shé, Eoghan Sheáin Eoghain,
Séamas Mhéine, Pádraig (na hInise) Ó Dála;
the remaining two people
in the photograph have not been identified.

George Chambers

George Chambers

An Island couple.
This house was built by
Tomás Ó Criomhthain
at some time after his marriage
in 1878.
It had two rooms:
a kitchen and a bedroom.
The census of 1901
records nine people living
in the two rooms.
This photograph,
taken in 1938,
shows Eibhlís Ní Shúilleabháin
and her husband
Seán Ó Criomhthain,
Tomás's son.
Eibhlís nursed Tomás
in his final years.
The couple's first child,
Niamh, is on her mother's lap.

An Island family.
Seán Mhicíl Ó Súilleabháin,
his wife, Siobhán Ní Dhuinnshlé,
one of their daughters,
Máire, and Pádraig,
Maidhc and Seáinín Mhicíl.

George Chambers

George Chambers

Eibhlís Ní Shúilleabháin.
She was to marry
Seán Ó Criomhthain.
This photograph,
taken in 1931,
shows Eibhlís at the age of twenty.
It was taken
by the Englishman George Chambers,
with whom she was to correspond
for twenty years.
A selection of her letters
was published
under the title
Letters from the Great Blasket (1978).

Island schoolchildren:
the Swedish folklorist
and ethnographer,
Carl Von Sydow,
visited the Island in 1924
and took a large collection
of photographs
of the Island community.
These are now preserved
in the Department of Irish Folklore,
University College, Dublin.

Carl Von Sydow

Happy boys:
Maidhc (Sheáisí) Ó Cearna
and Seán (Filí) Ó Cearna.
They must have been out
in a *naomhóg*
clearing lobster pots:
see the two lobsters at their feet.

Carl Von Sydow

Seán Pheats Taim Ó Cearna
and Mairéad
(Peig Bhofair) Ní Chatháin.

Carl Von Sydow

Three Ó Cearna children:
Eibhlín Pheats Taim,
Máire Pheats Taim
and Tomás Pheats Taim.
They all emigrated to America.

Carl Von Sydow

Bows in their hair.
Cáit (Sheáisí) Ní Chearna,
Cáit (Kate Filí) Ní Chearna,
Máire (Mary Filí) Ní Chearna,
and the last girl
has not been identified.

Carl Von Sydow

Carl Von Sydow

Island pinafores.
The younger girls
wore white pinafores.
Siobhán Ní Chearna and
perhaps Eibhlín (Neilí Pheig) Sayers:
the necklace is probably
a gift from Boston.

Carl Von Sydow

The older girls
wore dark or black pinafores.
Máire (Sheáisí) Ní Chearna,
Máire Pheats Taim Ní Chearna,
Peig (Bhofair) Ní Chatháin,
Siobhán (Hanna Pheats Taim) Ní Chearna,
Máire Mhaidhc Léan Ní Ghuithín,
Lís Savage,
Sissy Savage
(the schoolteacher's daughters);
to the front,
Cáit (Sheáisí) Ní Chearna,
Eibhlín Pheats Taim Ní Chearna,
Muiris Mhaidhc Léan Ó Guithín
and Treasa Savage.

Carl Von Sydow

Looking forward
to the time when he would have
his own *naomhóg*,
the young boy,
Mícheál (Maidhc Ghobnait) Ó Guithín,
is playing at rowing,
a popular game
amongst the Island's children.
His mother,
Gobnait Ní Chinnéide,
was a famous storyteller
who married into the Island.

Island women
coming down from Barr an Bhaile.

' ... I have a great mind to go to America ...
for Cáit Pheig is going
and I have no need to stay here
when all the girls
are departing ... '
(Twenty Years a-Growing).

The Island
was full of music
in the evenings
the young gathered
to dance and sing.

George Thomson

An Island task:
two of the young women
carry a hide container
of seaweed,
a sort of sea-lettuce,
to make a drink
called *sleadaí*.

Thomas Waddicor

Working in the Island fields:
'trenching' potato ridges.

Picking potatoes
on the Island.
The Island soil
gave good root crops:
the fields were manured
with seaweed.
Here Siobhán Ní Shúilleabháin
(*née* Ó Dhuinnshlé) and her daughter,
Eibhlís Ní Shúilleabháin
work in their field.

Carl Von Sydow

Thomas Waddicor

After mass
on a Sunday morning.
The community is returning
to their homes,
perhaps after mass
by a visiting priest
or after a boat journey
from the mainland at Dún Chaoin.
All are dressed in their best:
new caps, shawls.

Thomas Waddicor

Island visitors.
During the 1920s and 1930s,
right up to the second world war,
the Blasket Island was a centre for those
learning the Irish language
and for the study of Gaelic culture.
To the left of the Island postman
— Seán an Rí — is the Celtic scholar
Kenneth Jackson.
The house is that of
Máire Ní Ghuithín (Mary Pheats Mhicí
a daughter of the King
and brother of Seán an Rí).
She is standing to the right.

Portrait of an Island woman.
The crossover shawl
and the apron
indicate her married status.
I have always felt
that this Von Sydow photograph
is the most expressive
of his pictures.

Carl Von Sydow

Bringing home the turf
from the back of the Island.
This photograph was taken
about 1924.
In another ten years
the remaining turf on the Island
had been completely cut out,
leaving only furze
and heather for fuel:
it wasn't enough.

Carl Von Sydow

Caladh an Oileáin,
the Island harbour,
on a calm day.
An Trá Bhán can be seen
in the background;
a *naomhóg* with its crew
has just come in
from the mainland.

Tomás O Muircheartaigh

The village in its heyday.
There are *naomhóga*
right down to the breakwater
at Caladh an Oileáin.
Here at the bottom of the village
is the rest of
the Island fleet
with houses stretching up
from Bun an Bhaile
to the top at Barr an Bhaile.

Thomas Mason

The King's son, Seán an Rí,
the Island postman
and his wife Mairéad (Peig)
and one of their daughters.
Seán an Rí died in June 1934
leaving a very young family.

Thomas Waddicor

Moving livestock
out of the Island.
This was a most dangerous activity:
the cow, having been secured by rope,
had her legs tied,
and she then had to be laid
into the canvas covered frail boat.
Another *naomhóg* had
to follow
the first boat
in case of an accident.
Then, on arrival in Dún Chaoin,
the cow had to be taken out
of the *naomhóg*,
untied
and the animal transported to Dingle.

George Chambers

The *naomhóga*
at the lower part of the breakwater:
one *naomhóg*
carried by three of the Islanders
is carried down the slipway.
The oars on the right
under the cliff
and the number of boats,
calculated by three sea-going men
per boat in 1931,
and the five or six boats
up above, indicate an active fleet
of fifteen boats.

By the time this
second photograph
had been taken,
more of the *naomhóga* had been moved down
and out to the water.
Crouched men,
like the legs of beetles,
move their boats out,
drawing on the oars' supply.

George Chambers

The harbour at Dún Chaoin:
this was the base
for all movement in and out
of the Island.
It was from here
that the young Muiris Ó Súilleabháin
returned to the Island
for the first time.

George Chambers

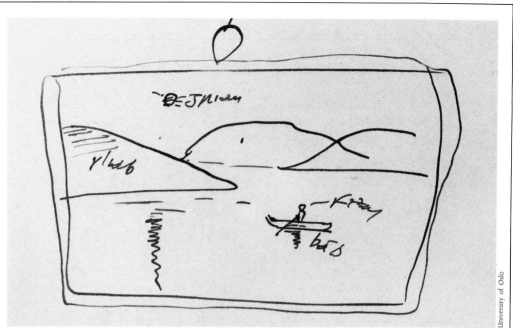

An Island landscape:
a sketch by Carl Marstrander
of the Island
with key words in Irish
as a learning aid:
sliabh (mountain),
grian (sun) are in the middle,
and *fear* (man) is rowing *bád* (boat).
This is from Marstrander's daybook
which he kept on the Blaskets
in 1907.

University of Oslo

An Islander with a hat.
A sketch by Carl Marstrander
of an Islander;
looking at early photographs
of Tomás Ó Criomhthain,
I believe the sketch to be of him.

University of Oslo

Carl Von Sydow

An Islander at a table:
furniture in the Island homes
was sparse
and confined to essential items.
Here in one of the 'new' houses
at Slinneán Bán,
at the top of the village,
Von Sydow photographed
a brother of the King,
Mícheál (Micí) Ó Catháin,
known as 'Bofar'.

V.Hjort

An Island kitchen:
since turf was scarce,
the fires were small
and had to provide heat
for living and for cooking.
White fish was smoked
above the fireplace.

Mother and daughter
in the Island.
One of the 'new' two-storied houses
at the top of the village
at Slinneán Bán.
Peig Ní Chatháin
and her mother
Máire Mháire Eoghain.

Carl Von Sydow

Siobhán Ní Chatháin (June Bhofair).
The furzewood for the fire
is on the floor
to her right.

Carl Von Sydow

A neolithic site:
the stone beehive hut to the left
was built about 120 years ago
as a grain store,
although it is built
in the *clochán* tradition
of two thousand years ago.
The outhouse to the right
is roofed in the
traditional manner with felt
or tarred canvas.
The buildings are at Bun an Bhaile,
bottom of the village.

Carl Von Sydow

Three Island houses:
the schoolhouse,
and below it the house
of Tom Ó Cearna,
and below it again
the house of Mícheál Cuainí Ó Catháin.
Beyond is Beiginis
and beyond that again
the mainland with
Ceann Sibéal to the left.

Thomas Mason

Two Island houses:
Máire Ní Ghuithín's house
is to the left:
here Robin Flower, Kenneth Jackson
and other visitors stayed.
Below Máire Ní Ghuithín's
was the house of An Rí,
where Synge, Marstrander and Flower,
on his first visit,
stayed.
When this photograph was taken,
the King had died
and his son, Seán an Rí,
is walking on the pathway
by his gable.
Behind these houses
can be seen
a sign of village decay:
a deserted house.

Thomas Waddicor

The village in early morning,
some time in the early 1930s.
The boats along the top of the cliff
(Barr a' Niúinigh)
tell how strong
the village then was:
even in the glare of the sun,
above the harbour
you can count eight *naomhóga*.

Tomás O Muircheartaigh

Eibhlín Ní Shúilleabháin
(Neilí Sheáin Lís),
sister of Muiris Ó Súilleabháin.
Brian Ó Ceallaigh
encouraged Eibhlín to
write a journal in Irish
which is now in
the National Library in Dublin.
Eibhlín went to America,
where she died young.

Robin Flower (Bláithín)
and Tomás Ó Criomhthain
(An tOileánach)
outside Tomás's house.

Carl Von Sydow

Thomas Mason

Thomas Mason

Tomás Ó Criomhthain
wrote his own account
of his life
and kept a daily journal:
they were published
in 1928 and 1929.

The Islandman and his house.
A rare photograph (1924)
of Tomás Ó Criomhthain
walking into his house.
Here he wrote the manuscripts
of An tOileánach and
Allagar na hInise.
It was in this house
that he died, in March 1937.

Carl Von Sydow

Carl Von Sydow

Tomás Ó Criomhthain:
the writer outside his own house
on the Great Blasket island
at Bun an Bhaile.
Tomás was then,
in 1924, seventy years of age.
He was over sixty
when he began to write
his Island journal.

Carl Von Sydow

An tOileánach,
the Islandman.
This is my favourite
portrait of Tomás Ó Criomhthain.
There is a recollection
of youth and vigour in his face,
although the writer was,
at this time,
seventy years of age.
Here is the fisherman
and seal-hunter,
writer and poet.

Caladh an Oileáin:
the building of the slipway
on the Island in 1910.
The foreman, John Corcoran,
was from Mayo
and had digs at the King's house.
The young man without a hat
is Robin Flower:
this is his first visit
to the Island.
He worked on the building
of the pier
and blistered his hands.
Tomás Ó Criomhthain
worked with Robin Flower
on the pier
and is standing beside him here.

Flower

The Islandman
in his seventies,
probably bored with
posing for photographs:
his journal had been published
in 1928 and his autobiography
in 1929.

George Chambers

Letter from an Island:
Carl Marstrander's draft
in Irish of a letter dated
from the village, 1907.

Carl Marstrander (1881-1965)
An Lochlannach.

Arán glas. leaves growing in the ... they are round like pennies.
Geamharcach, a kind of bulb with a few bare leaves and a ~~the~~ bluish flower, it was formerly used for tanning leather.
~~Fiorrach leaves growing in bunches in the clefts of rocks they are round like pennies.~~
Fiogán. bog-grass — long white grass used for making súgáin or hay-ropes.
Coinnle-copóg, a bulb growing in bogs; the stem is long, and its blossom is a lovely blue.
Cornrás, a plant with leaves something like carrots, having curative properties.
Raithneach. Ferns.
Fiorthan. long coarse grass.
Puirr-faille. long threads growing in cliffs, and producing a white flower.
~~Nóinín bán~~.
~~Noinín~~
Neoinín bán White daisy.
Neoinín buidhe Yellow daisy (primrose)
Glasair-léan. a blue plant growing in meadows
Fuilig. a soft green weed growing in potatoe gardens.
Aimeáin-gléurta. a plant with its leaves almost resembling the ivy – but not quite so smooth.
Praiseach buidhe. a yellow weed that grows in corn.
Blúcán. a plant like the millsóga mear – its roots are eaten and are sweet to the taste.
Slánlas. The lower leaves of the meadow-fox-tail; it has curative properties.
Raithneach madra. small-leaved fern.
Gabáiste faille. a wild plant with the leaves like cabbage, growing in the cliffs.
Greasdhuirc, long slender plants growing in rocks – sweet to taste.
Dealg. a thorn
Bainne-cíche-na-n-éan. hemlock.
Iorrach. an ever-green leafy tuft, that grows on mountains. it does not rise up, but spreads its leaves along the ground.
Cop-taos
Cuirliom
Préachán dubh
Préachán cos-dearg.
Crog. The

University of Oslo

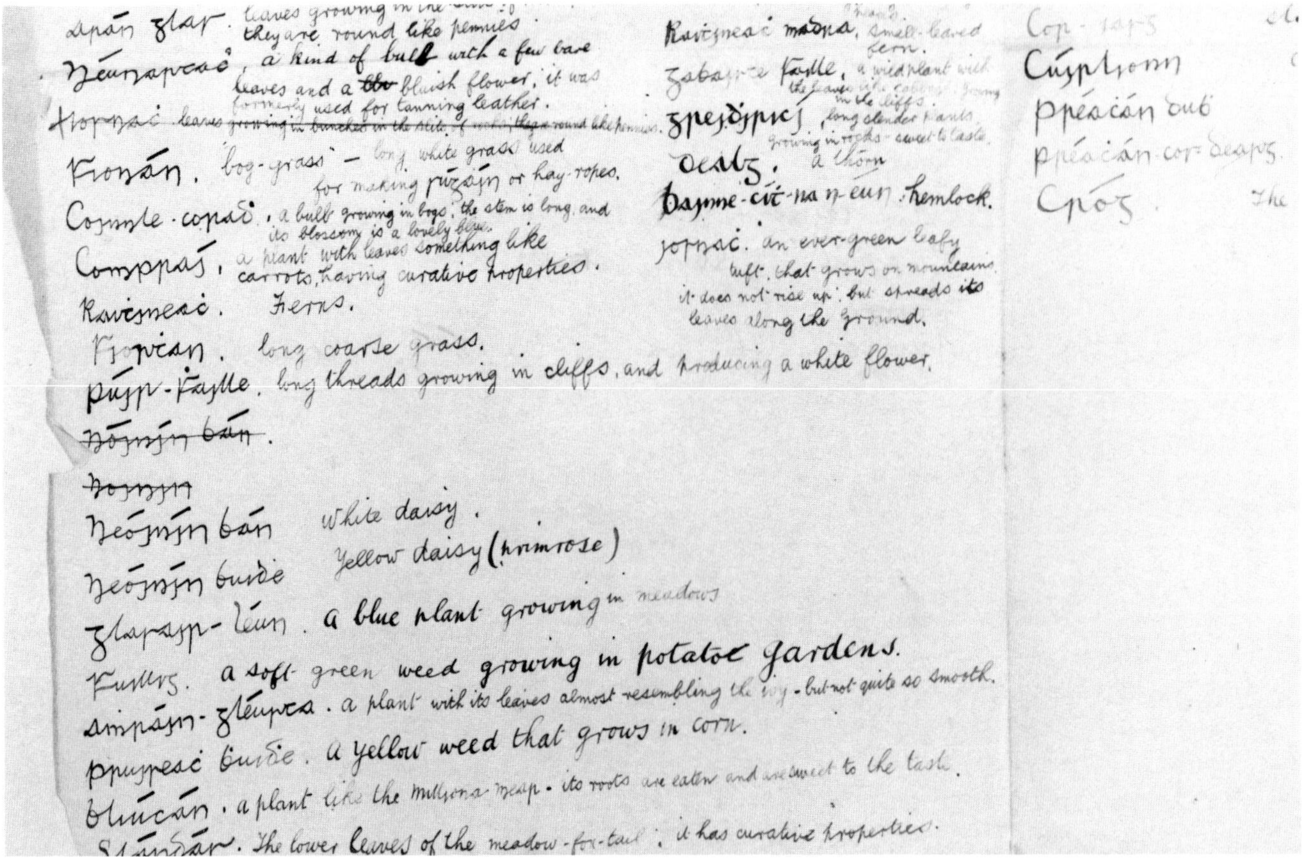

From Ó Criomhthain's postbag:
when the Norwegian scholar,
Carl Marstrander,
left the Island,
he asked Tomás to
compile a list of flora
and fauna for him.
Tomás did so with
the help of an Irish language teacher,
Tadhg Ó Ceallaigh.
These lists are preserved
in the Department of Celtic
at the Univeristy of Oslo.

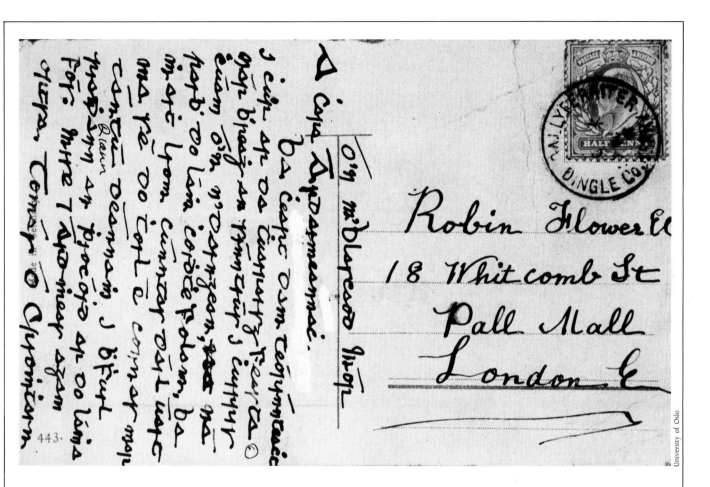

A postcard from Tomás
enquiring about the blisters
on Robin Flower's hands,
which had developed
after he had been working
on the new pier.

The scholar and two fishermen:
Robin Flower
meets two of the Island fishermen
at Bun an Bhaile.
In our picture
they exchange information
concerning the night's catch.

A visitor in the kitchen
in the early 1930s:
Robin Flower
with Máire Ní Ghuithín (Mary Pheats Mhicí)
and her daughter
Máire (Máire Mhaidhc Léain).

Robin Flower,
An Bláithín,
an older man.

Ida Mary Streeter,
Robin Flower's wife.
Flower brought his wife
to the Island
on their honeymoon in 1911.
She was a painter
and the drawings she made
on her honeymoon
adorn Flower's book
on the Island,
The Western Island.

Flower

Flower

Robin Flower with his son Patrick
on holidays in the Island.
Here they are
on the Island's white strand
An Trá Bhán.

Robin Flower as a young man.
This is how Flower must have looked
when he met
Tomás Ó Criomhthain
for the first time in 1910.

Flower

Robin Flower,
scholar and friend
of the Blasket Islanders.
Flower in his writings
and lectures
identified the cultural importance
of the Island:
other scholars followed him.

Muiris Ó Súilleabháin
and his grandfather
Daideo Eoghan.

George Thomson

The scholarly Englishman
George Thomson,
Seoirse Mac Tomáis,
who came to the Island
on the advice of Robin Flower.

Thomas Waddicor

A return to the Island:
Muiris Ó Súilleabháin (left,
wearing hat) and George Thomson (top right)
on the slipway
at Caladh an Oileáin.

Muiris Ó Súilleabháin
at the breakwater
at Caladh an Oileáin.

Muiris Ó Súilleabháin
in Peig Sayers's house
at Slinneán Bán
at the top of the village,
1924.

Carl Von Sydow

Peig Sayers
at Baile Viocáire, Dún Chaoin.
Peig left the Island
in 1942 with her son
Mícheál and her brother-in-law,
another Mícheál.

Caoimhín O Danachair

Caoimhín Ó Danachair

Peig Sayers at home
in Baile Viocáire
on the mainland.

Máirín Feiritéar

Island visitors:
Peig enjoyed meeting visitors.
Here on the bank
outside her house
at Slinneán Bán
she entertains two young scholars,
Nessa Ní Shé (Bean Í Dheoráin)
and Caitríona MacLeod.
Mícheál Ó Guithín,
her brother-in-law,
is on the right.

Peig Sayers
and her daughter Eibhlín (Neilí).
This picture
was taken by Von Sydow
in 1924 outside Peig's house
at the top of the village.

Carl Von Sydow

Her daughter Neilí
went to America (Boston)
where she married
and still lives.

Peig Sayers
in her early sixties.
Her hair had originally been blond
and she was known
as Peig Bhuí (blonde Peig).
She was a very beautiful woman
in her younger days.

Mícheál Ó Gaoithín,
the Island poet.
Son of Peig Sayers,
the Islanders called him
Maidhc File ·· Mike the poet.

Thomas Waddicor

Thomas Waddicor

Maidhc Pheig Sayers
(Maidhc File) in 1924.
We can't identify
the young woman knitting
and her children.

Carl Von Sydow

Peig Sayers, now blind,
in Dingle hospital
with her son
Mícheál (Maidhc File).

Tomás Ó Muircheartaigh

Peig in hospital,
with the poet Seán Ó Ríordáin
(1916-1977).

Tomás Ó Muircheartaigh

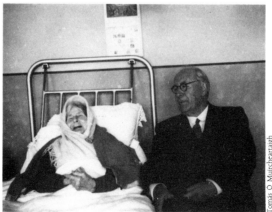

Peig in Dingle hospital
with An Seabhac (1883-1964),
writer, publisher and editor.
An Seabhac edited
the first versions
of Tomás Ó Criomhthain's
journal and autobiogrpahy.

Tomás Ó Muircheartaigh

Eibhlís (Lís) Ní Shúilleabháin.
She wrote a series
of letters over twenty years
which gives a most interesting
picture of Island life.
The letters were to
the Englishman, George Chambers,
who took this photograph
in 1931.

George Chambers

Eibhlís (Lís) Ní Shúilleabháin,
wife of Seán Ó Criomhthain,
carrying water
home from the well.

Seán Ó Criomhthain
and his wife
Eibhlís Ní Shúilleabháin
in 1938.

George Chambers

Thomas Waddicor.

Carl Von Sydow

Seán Ó Criomhthain
at home in 1924.
Seán was the last surviving son
of Tomás Ó Criomhthain.
He married
Eibhlís Ní Shúilleabháin in 1933
and buried his father in 1937.
Seán and his family
were to move to the mainland
at Muiríoch
to the north of Ballyferriter
in 1942.
Seán wrote an important account
of the last days of the Island
and of the new life
on the mainland.

Rí an Oileáin,
the King of the Island,
Pádraig Ó Catháin,
on a path above the village in 1905.

J.M. Synge

This photograph
and some others were taken by
John Millington Synge
during his visit to the Island,
when he stayed in the house of An Rí.
These photographs by Synge
are probably the first ones
to have been taken on the Great Blasket.

The Island King
and a group of Islanders
taken by Synge in 1905.

J.M. Synge

From left:
Mícheál (Bofar) Ó Catháin,
Mícheál Ó Guithín,
Tomás Ó Duinnshlé,
Séamas Ó Duinnshlé,
Muiris Ó Catháin,
Pádraig Ó Catháin (An Rí)
and his daughter Cáit.
The young girls are probably
the daughters of Mícheál Ó Catháin,
Neilí and Máire;
the young boy
has not been identified.

Cáit Ní Chatháin (An Princess),
daughter of the Island King,
Pádraig Ó Catháin
and her little cousin,
Máire Ní Chatháin.
Cáit was not married when Synge
took this photograph.
She eventually married
out of the Island
on the mainland in Baile an Teampaill.
Her husband was Seán Ó Cathasa.

J.M. Synge

A class of converts

This is a pencil on paper drawing (18cm x 22cm). The heads are very carefully drawn from life. The seven figures are identified by number and the details were inscribed on the back of the drawing as follows:

A sketch of a class of the converts as they were being examined at Ventry 8th Aug[ust], 1842.

1. Gloster schoolmaster at Donquin. [The surname Glouster was and is known in the area, particularly to the north of the parish of Ballyferriter at Baile na nGall and Feothanach. James Glouster was probably teaching in Carraig before becoming a member of the Protestant faith.]

2. John Sullivan Irish Reader at the Blasket Island. [John Sullivan was the first teacher in the Protestant school on the Island and may have been a brother of Mícheál Ó Súilleabháin, one of the two Island poets of the nineteenth century, and one of the first Islanders to join the Protestant faith.]

3. Dan Sullivan Irish Reader at Ventry he underwent very great persecuition when he [first] read the script[ures]. His own brother waylaid him to beat him, we were shown a hole in the ditch where he was obliged to hide his Irish Test[ament] lest it sh[ould] be burnt.

4. Tom Connor Irish Reader at Ventry.

5. Tom Kennedy Irish Reader at Ventry formerly the parish piper & in comparative affluence, but reduced to distress and poverty on his conversion.

[Tomás Ó Cinnéide, 'Cinnéidí an píobaire', lived at Carraig and was an outstanding piper with an extensive repertoire. Ó Cinnéide was a friend of the Reverend James (Séamas) Goodman (1826-96), born near Dingle and later to become Professor of Irish at Trinity College Dublin. Goodman collected a considerable number of tunes from Ó Cinnéide and these form part of the Goodman collection in Trinity College, which have not as yet been published.]

6. Jordan the Schoolmaster at Ventry. [James Jordan lived with his wife and their children on the Island and taught in the Protestant school which, in the late 1840s, was attended by the children of those families on the Island who had become Protestants.]
These men are employed by the Ladies Aux[iliary] or *Readers'* Branch of the Irish Soc[iety] w[ho] is responsible for the expenses of the Readers, Schoolmaster, orphans & widows & at Ventry & Donquin.

7. An interesting oldman whose scrip[ture] knowledge tho' lately acquired surprised us very much.

Similar sketches will be sold for the benefit of the Readers' Branch of the Irish Socty.

Signed Wm Mulready, R.A. [For a variety of reasons the attribution to the artist William Mulready cannot be so and the writing on the back of the drawing is not that of Mulready.]

National Gallery of Ireland, Cat. No. 7808

Tuesday, 17 November 1953,
the day appointed
for the final evacuation
of the Island.
A *naomhóg*
makes its way out
from the Island
with some of the evacuees.
Walter McGrath,
a reporter with
the *Cork Examiner*,
wrote in his report
the following day:
'Yesterday was the day fixed
for the final exodus,
but the weather
decreed otherwise,
and only six
out of twenty-one
were able to leave the Island
owing to the huge swell
in the rolling seas.'

Louis McMonagle/*Cork Examiner*

The Island *naomhóg*
draws away
from the evacuating trawler,
the *Naomh Lorcáin Ó Tuathail*
from Dingle.
The land commission official,
Dan O'Brien,
had to get the Islanders
to sign the papers
for the transfer to the mainland.

Louis McMonagle/*Cork Examiner*

PART II

CHAPTER 1

Tomás Ó Criomhthain
and Outside Influences

This then was the world of the Blasket Islander and it was from within this world that the writer Tomás Ó Criomhthain emerged. His story is pivotal to the story of the Blaskets and its culture.

We do not have the precise date of Tomás Ó Criomhthain's birth, as registration of births, deaths and marriages was not compulsory in Ireland until 1864. He himself suggested to the editor of the first edition of his autobiography *An tOileánach* that he was born on Saint Thomas's day in the year 1856, but the record of Tomás Ó Criomhthain's baptism in the parish church at Ballyferriter shows that he was baptised on 29 April 1855. The feast of Saint Thomas the Apostle falls on 21 December, and it is possible that Tomás was born on that date in the year 1854. However, such a long delay between birth and baptism would have been quite unusual. It is unlikely that Tomás was named in honour of the saint, a saint unknown in the area. Tomás was probably a family name: the sponsors to Tomás Ó Criomhthain's baptism were a Tomás and Bríd Ó Criomhthain, and the writer probably owes his name to his godfather. The Saint Thomas connection may have arisen as a result of the interest of the first editor of *An tOileánach*.

Tomás Ó Criomhthain was born, in my view, in April 1855. He was the son of Dónal Ó Criomhthain and Cáit Ní Shé and was the last of their eight children to be baptised. His father, who married into the Blaskets on 26 January 1837, was born in November 1808 in Márthain on the mainland, the son of Conchúr Ó Criomhthain and Cáit Ní Chonchúir. The Ó Criomhthain name had its origins in the great Mac Criomhthain family who were leaders in the barony to the south of Corca Dhuibhne across Dingle Bay in Uíbh Ráthach. What brought Tomás's ancestors across the bay we do not know, but in the aftermath of the confederate wars and the Desmond uprising many of the great families were uprooted and dispersed.

Tomás's eldest surviving sister, Máire, was eleven years older than he and the next youngest, Nóra, was at least three years at his birth. As the youngest, he was treated as the pet of the family. His father, for whom he had great admiration, particularly as a craftsman and fisherman, was, as he describes him, a 'strong thick-set man', while his mother was 'easily as tall as a policeman'.

The house in which Tomás was reared was small and narrow with a thatch roof of rushes in which a hen frequently had a nest with twelve eggs. The house had a settle bed and two other beds at the lower end. All the animals — cows, pigs and fowl, as well as a donkey — were housed indoors at night along with Tomás, his parents, his brother and sisters.

The medium of instruction was at that time English and when Tomás left school he could both read and write English, but was illiterate in Irish. Until quite recently most of the population of the Irish-speaking areas were unable to read or write in Irish, their own language. Tomás was well over forty when he acquired a reading and writing capacity in Irish.

Like any young man on the Island, he began to prepare himself for the course of life and to equip himself with the skills of fishing and seal hunting, the basis of the Island livelihood. Tomás acquired from his father those skills and the craft of masonry, which were to stand to his stead right to the end of his life.

Like most young men Tomás also turned to thoughts of love and his description in his autobiography of his courtship of a young girl from Inis Icíleáin is a moving one. The account of the courtship covers several visits to the Inis mostly in the company of Tomás's uncle, Diarmaid. They went there hunting rabbits, but the Inis family — muintir Dhála — were also renowned for their hospitality. Diarmaid, a brother of Tomás's mother, was married to a sister of the wife of Dálach na hInise. Diarmaid may have sensed the prospect of a match and also perhaps of a drink! Tomás and Diarmaid had a marvellous time on the several visits, during which they danced and sang in the Dála house at Log na bhFiolar. Tomás was quite taken with one of the daughters of the house and they left the revelry on a number of occasions to be alone.

On one occasion both visitors and those on the Inis went hunting rabbits:

Lá aoibhinn a b'ea é, coiníní ag imeacht agus madraí ina ndiaidh, iad ag breith ar cheann agus dhá cheann ag tabhairt na gcos uathu. Ach is i dtreo na n-ógbhan a chaitheas féin an tráthnóna, agus bhí a rian air, níor mhór í mo sheilg.

D'fhilleamar ar an dtigh agus tháinig Diarmaid agus Kerry isteach, agus gan de Kerry le feiscint ach a dhá shúil, bhí a oiread sin coiníní thiar ar a dhrom aige.

It was a beautiful day, rabbits running and dogs after them catching one and two getting away. However it was with the young women that I spent the evening which was obvious because of the size of my catch.

We returned to the house and Diarmaid and Kerry [another hunter] came in, only Kerry's two eyes could be seen with the amount of rabbits on his back.

'Mo ghraidhin do chroí, a sheanuncail,' arsa mise le Diarmaid. 'Ar m'anam gur tusa an fiagaí agus nach mise, gan agam ach dosaen ó mhaidin.'

'Dar Mhuire, a chroí, is maith a bhí a fhios agamsa nár mhór na coiníní a thitfeadh leatsa nuair a chonac i bhfochair ma mban óg ar maidin thú,' arsa Diarmaid.

'Good man, old uncle,' said I to Diarmaid. 'Truly you are the hunter and not I with only a dozen since morning.'

'I knew very well, old stock, that you would not account for many rabbits when I saw you with the young women this morning.'

Tomás Ó Criomhthain goes out of his way in his autobiography to make it quite clear that the Inis Icíleáin girl was the centre of his life:

... níorbh fhada go raibh ceann acu agus mé féin ag síorshúgradh le chéile, cailín deas breá, an t-amhránaí ba bhreátha a bhí ar siúl lena linn ...

... it wasn't long before one of them the girls and myself were constantly flirting with one another, a nice fine girl, the best singer of her time ...

It was very evident that both Tomás and the girl were moving towards marriage. This was not to be, however much Diarmaid, his uncle, urged the marriage on Tomás's parents.

When Tomás came to write his autobiography he wrote an account of a departure from the Inis after three days of rabbit hunting and the Ó Dála hospitality. Everybody on Inis Icíleáin accompanied the hunters to the water's edge:

... ní raibh fead ná glao acu toisc sinn a bheith á bhfágaint. Níl gnó agam agamsa a rá ná gur chailleas féin mo chuid suilt, pé duine eile a chaill é, mar dheineas go cruinn, ní hiontas sin, agus mé ag scarúint leis an tamall grinn is mó a bhuail riamh liom, agus ina theannta sin mé ag tabhairt mo chúil leis an ógbhean ba thaitneamhaí a bhí ar an dtalamh naofa san am sin.

... they neither whistled or called because of our departure from them. I mustn't say that I did not lose my sense of happiness, whoever else lost it, for I did just that, not surprisingly since I was leaving the greatest moment of pleasure which I had ever encountered, and in addition to that I was turning my back on the fondest young woman in the whole world then.

Tomás's elder sister Máire had been married to Mártan Ó Catháin, a son of the then Island king, in 1862: the couple had one child and Máire was widowed not long afterwards. It appears that Máire and her young son had to return to the Ó Criomhthain house: her brother-in-law claimed his own brother's property. Máire went to America and returned with funds to undertake a court action against her brother-in-law and to claim her son's inheritance. She prosecuted successfully according to Tomás's account.

What is interesting about this story and Tomás's love for the Inis Icíleáin girl is that from his account of the affair it was his sister Máire, now remarried, who intervened in the process. She suggested to her parents that their interests and those of Tomás would be better served if Tomás were not to marry the girl from the Inis and move there, but to remain on the Great Blasket and marry Máire Ní Chatháin, a niece of her first husband. The arranged marriage must have been part of a wider agreement concerning the affairs of the two families and Máire Ní Chriomhthain's settlement. Máire Ní Chatháin and Tomás Ó Criomhthain were married in Ballyferriter on 5 February 1878: they were second cousins once removed.

Tomás gives us an indication of what the whole affair meant to him, the girl on the Inis and his marriage to Máire, when he says that he sang one song at his wedding. Tomás was a man who loved to sing and hear others sing as well. He also included the words of many songs which he and the other Islanders performed in his writing. Tomás was a 'singer of tales' and singing is an important characteristic of his.

Tomás tells us in the account of his marriage which he gives in his autobiography that he chose to sing 'Caisleán Í Néill'. It was a curious choice, to say the least, for a newly wed: a love poem about broken hearts:

Mo shlán chun na hoíche aréir, is mo léan nach í anocht atá ann,

Mo bhuachaillín séimh deas a bhréagfadh mé seal ar a ghlún

Dá neosfainn mo scéal duit is baolach ná déanfá orm rún

Go bhfuil mo ghrá bán dom thréigean, is a Dhia ghléigil is a Mhuire nach dubhach.

Farewell to last night, I am sorry that it's not tonight

My tender lovely boy who would coax me upon his knee

If I told you my story I'm afraid you would not keep it

That my dear love is forsaking me, o dear God and Mary is it not sad.

Thus it was that Tomás Ó Criomhthain, a young man of some twenty-three years, entered into the most onerous part of his life. A household had to be established and a house built; there were two mouths to feed, with obligations also to his parents and the preparations necessary for the arrival in time of a young family.

During the period of Tomás's marriage the fishing economy of the Island moved from the heavy seine boats to the use of the *naomhóg*, the small canvas-covered canoe and to the fishing of lobster and crayfish. The Dingle fishermen had already entered the field before the Islanders, with considerable success. Foreign trawlers from Brittany, the Isle of Man and Spain were both fishing in the area and buying the Islanders' catches. The housing also changed. The Island's houses were gradually reroofed with tarred canvas, felt or timber.

Tomás built a new house for his family, and this was to be his abode for the rest of his long life. The remains of the house, unroofed and opened to the skies, still stand at Bun an Bhaile with An Trá Bhán at its back. Although I have stood inside the house on many occasions, I always find it difficult to conjure up the house as it was when Tomás was alive. The census of 1901, taken on the Island on the last day of March of that year, records that the Ó Criomhthain house was a third-class house, as were almost all his neighbours' houses, having stone walls, a perishable roof (timber and felt) and two windows to the front of the house. There were nine occupants, including Máire, Tomás's wife, who, according to the census, could neither read, write nor speak English. There were five sons — Pádraig, eighteen years, described as a fisherman, Tomás, fourteen years, still at school, as were Dónal, ten years, Muiris, five years, and Seán, three years — and two daughters — Eibhlín, sixteen years, and Cáit, twelve years — who were both at school.

The census for 1911, ten years later, records the Ó Criomhthain household as still being roofed with a perishable roof, but there was an additional window, three outhouses and five inhabitants, composed of three sons — Pádraig, Muiris and Seán, the younger two of whom were still at school. There was also Tomás's brother Pádraig (who had returned from the United States) and Tomás himself: both Tomás and his brother were described as widowers. While Tomás signed his name in English on the 1901 census as Thomas Crohan, he signed the 1911 form as Tomás Ó Criomhthain, the only signature in Irish in that census on the Blaskets.

The loss of members of Tomás's family was gradual but definite. Tomás lost a son hunting seagulls. Then a whooping cough epidemic scoured the Island and Tomás spent three months nursing his children, two of whom died in that epidemic. Their deaths hastened the death of his wife Máire. Another son, Dónal, was drowned while trying to save Cáit, his sister and Tomás's youngest daughter, and Eveleen Nicholls, a visitor friend of the family. The two girls had been swimming off An Trá Bhán. Cáit survived and Eveleen Nicholls drowned. She was a friend of Patrick Pearse and there is a strong tradition in the Island that Pearse came to Dún Chaoin for the funeral. That funeral was one of the largest ever in Dún Chaoin, and the circumstances of the drowning were reported widely in the national newspapers.

So, by 1911 Tomás had three sons at home and his brother. Cáit had married in Dún Chaoin and Eilín had gone to America. Some time after that census the eldest son, Pádraig, injured himself when he fell carrying a *naomhóg* and died shortly afterwards and was buried with Dónal. Cáit died giving birth to her seventh child. Muiris, the second youngest, went to the United States, returning once with his wife and family in August 1920. He stayed for six months and returned to the States upon realising that all that had been saved in America would be spent without the chance of earning anything on the Island. That left Tomás with one son at home, Seán, the youngest boy. He was to marry eventually, on the Island, and was one of the last to leave.

If this seems a grim recital of bleak events, it does not give by any means the full flavour of Tomás Ó Criomhthain's extraordinary life. But this list of tragedies is not an unusual one for an Island family. Other Islanders had to suffer similarly from infant mortality, virus infections, 'flu, whooping cough, melancholia, TB, meningitis and the ordinary physical injuries and drownings which arose from their island location. In the Ireland of the nineteenth and early twentieth century immunisation and medical care were a rarity.

Tomás Ó Criomhthain lived his life on the sea as did the other men of the Island, hunting seals and fishing, often in dangerous conditions, and he frequently spent his time on the sea at night in his *naomhóg*, waiting to lift nets. Occasionally he brought his catch to the mainland to sell in Dingle and even went further afield, to Caherciveen in Uíbh Ráthach for that purpose. Sometimes, when weatherbound on the mainland, he would stay at the house of a relative in Baile Ícín, Dún Chaoin. In the 1890s the Irish language was introduced as a subject in the national school curriculum and special provisions were made in the case of schools in the Gaeltacht that some of the teaching could be conducted in the communities' own language. Irish was being taught at the national school at Dún Chaoin from the last decade of the nineteenth century. It happens that the household in which Tomás stayed had school-going children, and during the winter months and when stormbound, Tomás began to learn to read and write in Irish from the school primers of the children of the household. The house belonged to Seán Ó Muircheartaigh, who was married to a relative of Tomás, Neill Ní Criomhthain, and Seán Ó Muircheartaigh (Seán a' Scraiste) may also have had manuscripts in Irish in the house. The result was that Tomás Ó Criomhthain learned to read and later to write Irish when he was over forty years of age.

While Tomás had to live out his hard life on the Island, a change in attitudes towards the fortunes of the Irish language in the outside world was to open up the world of Tomás Ó Criomhthain and those of his neighbours. With the gradual recognition throughout Europe of the importance of the Celtic languages and their literatures and with the language revival movement in Ireland, the village on the Great Blasket island was to become for a short and critical time a centre for those seeking both the living language and its culture.

This wave of recognition for the Irish language and its culture brought the young John Millington Synge to the Island in August 1905. He was the first of the literary and scholarly visitors. Synge's account of his visit to the Island gives us an interesting description of the house of An Rí:

This cottage where I am to stay is one of the highest of the group, and as we passed up to it through little paths among the cottages many, white-wolfish looking dogs came out and barked furiously. My host had gone on in front with my bag, and when I reached his threshold he came forward and shook hands with me again, with a finished speech of welcome. His eldest daughter, a young married woman of about twenty, who manages the house, shook hands with me also, and then, without asking if we were hungry, began making us tea in a metal teapot and frying rashers of bacon. She is a small, beautifully-formed woman, with brown hair and eyes — instead of the black hair and blue eyes that are usually found with this type in Ireland — and delicate feet and ankles that are not common in these parts, where the woman's work is so hard.

I am afraid that the Islanders took offence at some of Synge's remarks both in the passage quoted above and from other passages in his account. They must have read his material when it was first published in *The Shanachie* (An Irish Miscellany, Dublin, 1906-7) or heard about his writing after the 'Playboy riots' and the attack by the Gaelic League on his work. Their relatives in Boston and New York were also a factor in the view of Synge; there was constant correspondence between the Islanders at home and in America.

The reference to the provision of the tea and the rashers of bacon 'without asking if we were hungry' is still alive in the Islanders' memory eighty years after the event. The daughter of the young 'beautifully-formed woman' remembers that her mother told her in response to the Synge comment:

... bhuel, fear a bhí taréis teacht isteach ó Dhún Chaoin, déarfá go b'ea bheadh áthas air, sin é an nós a bhí san Oileán, dheintí, ní deirtí faic, 'An mbeidh tae ná faic agat?' ach an tae a dhéanamh ... dúirt sí ná raibh an méid a scríg sé i gceart ...

... well, a man who had just come in from Dún Chaoin, you'd say that he would be happy, that was the practice in the Island, it would be made, nothing would be said, 'Will you have tea or something?' but the tea would be made ... she said that what he wrote was not correct ...

If the Islanders were touchy about this episode, Synge's account of the condition of the house of An Rí and the dress and attire of the young women and the children upset them also. As Synge is about to go to bed around eleven o'clock

... the little hostess lighted a candle, carried it into the room beyond the kitchen, and stuck it up on the end of the bedpost of one of the beds with a few drops of grease. Then she took off her apron, and fastened it up in the window as a blind, laid another apron on the wet earthen floor for me to stand on, and left me to myself.

I have always thought Synge's account of his sojourn on the Island to be most carefully written and sensitive to the Island culture. Some of my friends from the Blaskets disagree. It is evident that the young woman — Máire Ní Chatháin (Mary Pheats Mhicí), 'my little hostess' — made an impression on him as the several references to her reveal already. Synge wrote a poem about her:

On an Island

You've plucked a curlew, drawn a hen,
Washed the shirts of seven men,
You've stuffed my pillow, stretched the sheet,
And filled the pan to wash your feet,
You've cooped the pullets, wound the clock,
And rinsed the young men's drinking crock;
And now we'll dance to jigs and reels,
Nailed boots chasing girls' naked heels.
Until your father'll start to snore,
And Jude, now you're married, will stretch on the floor.

The 'little hostess', Máire Ní Chatháin, was to play an important role in Synge's work for she was the prototype for Pegeen Mike in *The Playboy of the Western World*.

Synge took a small collection of photographs during his stay on the Island, probably the first photographs to be taken on the Blaskets. Synge's camera was a Klito which used plates. There are five photographs from Synge's Blasket visit. Included in the pictures are Pádraig Ó Catháin, the King, and one of his daughters, Cáit, a sister of Synge's 'little hostess'.

It must have been Synge who introduced the Blasket Islands to the consciousness of writers like W.B. Yeats and James Joyce. Yeats, for instance, writing *Oedipus*, hoped that his work would result in 'a plain man's Oedipus' which would be 'intelligible on the Blasket Island'. Joyce, according to his biographer Richard Ellmann, drew on a story which he heard about the Blaskets when discussing the death of his father and the notion of filial piety with the French academician Louis Gillet. The story is an interesting one and I have not heard it told in relation to the Island. Apparently an old Islander went to the mainland and bought a small mirror at a fair. The Islander had never seen a mirror before and brought it back to the Island. While rowing back he looked at the mirror occasionally murmuring, 'Oh Papa! Papa!'. He would not show it to his wife, but she soon became aware of his having some secret. On a hot day, when both were at work in the fields, he hung his jacket on a hedge. She saw her chance, rushed to the jacket and seized the cherished object. But when she looked at the mirror, she cried, 'Ach, it's nothing but an old woman!' and angrily threw it down so that it broke upon a stone. Richard Ellmann said that the story suited Joyce because it allocated filial piety to men and vanity to women.

Synge drew on the Island culture and introduced it to those Irish writers working in English but drawing from the Irish 'Gaelic' tradition.

Lady Gregory reported to Yeats, in relation to the proposal that Synge be appointed organiser of an Irish language theatre, that Synge 'has a plan for bringing a Gaelic company from the Blasket Islands ... Synge would stage manage it himself'. Synge, in the midst of the row with the famed Miss Horniman of the Abbey Theatre, even contemplated that, in the event of failure, he would 'go and live the rest of my natural life with the king of the Blasket Islands'. Alas, Synge died too soon for that.

Although Synge had a grasp of the Irish language and understood its importance, he felt committed to writing of the community's experience in English: he wrote, however sympathetically, with the eye and ear of an outsider. Fortunately for the Blasket island community, when the issue of creating their own literature arose, they chose to write in their own language and not to follow Synge. This decision by the Blasket Islanders to write in their own language rather than in English was influenced by the number of scholar visitors who followed Synge to the Island. The first of these was Carl Marstrander.

Carl Marstrander (1881-1965), a Norwegian linguistics scholar, came into the Island in the late summer of 1907 to learn modern Irish. Marstrander stayed in the King's house and was directed to Tomás by the King. They established a pupil-teacher relationship. Marstrander stayed on the Island for some five months and Tomás Ó Criomhthain worked with the young Norwegian scholar for two or three hours a day for the five months. Marstrander brought with him a newly published novel in Irish, *Niamh* (1907), by Father Peadar Ó Laoghaire, a writer of the Irish language revival movement whose prose style contributed to the development of a modern idiom for the Irish language. It was a happy coincidence that Ó Criomhthain should be introduced both at the same time to the young Norwegian scholar and to the work of a writer in Irish who was to establish the direction for prose in modern Irish.

The Islanders took Marstrander to their hearts and they gave him the petname of 'An Lochlannach' — the Viking. Marstrander was a strong man. He had been a pole-vault champion in his own country and should have joined the Norwegian Olympic team in Athens, for which he had been selected, were it not for his pursuit of the Irish language on the Island. To prove his prowess, Marstrander once vaulted over Tomás's house using one of the oars of an Island *naomhóg*. He worked with the

Islanders on land and on sea and thus he acquired a real grasp of the living language: he became one of the community.

Marstrander gives us an insight into the way in which he acquired the language through his relationship with the people of the Island. A draft letter in Irish found among his papers in Oslo, dated from the Blaskets on 15 September 1907, contains the following:

Bím in éineacht leotha mar bheadh duine acu féinig agus is mar sin is fearr sin do dhuine atá tagtha ag triall orthu ag foghlaim na teanga atá uaidh: agus ní miste dhom rá go bhfuilim ag dul i bhfeabhas go cuíosach. D'fhéadfainn anois cheana gach rud is maith liom fhéin a chur in iúl sa Ghaelinn agus táim sásta mar gheall air, mar ná raibh aon fhocal nach mór agam nuair a d'fhágas B.A.C.

I'm in their company with them as one of themselves and that is the best way for someone who has come to them to learn the language from them: and I don't mind saying that I'm improving moderately. I could now express what I wish in Irish, which pleases me for I had hardly any word when I left Dublin.

Marstrander returned to Oslo where he had won a scholarship in comparative linguistics and continued his work on Irish. Marstrander stayed in touch with Tomás Ó Criomhthain for a while and wrote to him on one occasion seeking a list of the Irish names of the Blasket flora and fauna. Tomás compiled the list with the help of an Irish language teacher who was visiting the Island at the time and sent it off, and this list is preserved amongst the Marstrander papers in the Univeristy of Oslo.

Marstrander came back to Ireland in 1910 to teach at the School of Irish Learning and in the following year to undertake the editing of the *Dictionary of the Irish Language*. His task was an onerous one and he also had to work against a deadline of two years. Marstrander produced studies on the history of the Norse language in Ireland (1915), the Norse language in the Isle of Man (1932), the Gaelic dialects of the Isle of Man and Scotland and the Breton language. He was a Norwegian nationalist who followed the plight of Ireland during the Easter 1916 rising and enquired about the fate of Eoin MacNeill. He was imprisoned himself by the Nazis in his own country.

While Marstrander's work on the dictionary was in progress, he became ill, with pleurisy, in the early spring of 1911. Tomás Ó Criomhthain received a postcard from him indicating that an operation was necessary. Tomás wrote to Robin Flower, Marstrander's student, expressing concern about the health of his friend. The operation at Sir Patrick Dun's Hospital brought Marstrander to recuperate at Monte Carlo: a long, long way from the Island.

Tomás Ó Criomhthain remembered An Lochlannach, Carl Johan Sverdrup Marstrander, until his dying day, and is recorded as saying of him: 'Ní fear go dtí é — There wasn't a man like him.' Marstrander's decision to come to the Blaskets to learn Irish, his mastery of it in such a short time, his time spent working with the Island community and his friendship with Tomás and regard for the quality of Tomás's Irish, were all factors which convinced Tomás and the other Islanders that theirs was an important culture and that there was a future for the Island writer in Irish.

With the visit of Marstrander, the world began to open up for Tomás. On his return to Dublin Marstrander was appointed to teach Old Irish and comparative philology at the recently established School of Irish Learning in Dublin. A young English scholar from the British Museum, one Robin Flower, came to the school to learn Old Irish with Marstrander. Once the contact with Marstrander had been made, a visit to the Blaskets was inevitable. Marstrander urged the young Englishman to go to Tomás Ó Criomhthain and take lessons from the master.

Robin Flower made his way south to Tralee by train and then took the narrow-gauge railway from Tralee to Dingle and then by pony and trap to Dún Chaoin. Then came a sea voyage by *naomhóg* into the Island, where he was to stay at the house of An Rí and to meet his future teacher Tomás Ó Criomhthain:

The kitchen gradually empties ... but a sudden feeling comes upon you of a new presence in the room. You look up and see, leaning against the wall almost with the air of being magically materialised out of nothing, a slight but confident figure. The face takes your attention at once and holds it.

This face is dark and thin, and there look out of it two quick and living eyes, the vivid witnesses of a fine and self-sufficient intelligence ... This is Tomás Ó Criomhthain, the Island poet and storyteller ...

Robin Flower (1881-1946) was born at Meanwood, near Leeds in Yorkshire, and read classics at Pembroke College, Oxford, before joining the manuscripts department at the British Museum in 1906. The British Museum has an extensive collection of manuscripts in the Irish language and it fell to Flower to complete the cataloguing of the collection. Flower realised that it would be necessary for him to acquire a working knowledge of the Irish language, both Old and Modern Irish. The British Treasury made a grant of 15 to Flower to enable him to come to Dublin to attend the Marstrander lectures, but the Blasket venture was not covered by the Treasury's munificence.

When Robin Flower came to the Island for the first time in 1910 he was twenty-nine years of age: Tomás was then fifty-five. The Congested Districts Board was engaged in a series of works on the Island: the construction of the breakwater at Caladh an Oileáin, the repair and extension of the Island roads and the building of new two-storey houses at Slinneán Bán up at the back of the village.

Tomás Ó Criomhthain and Robin Flower worked together on the road-making and on the construction of the slipway at Caladh an Oileáin during Flower's first visit to the Island. Flower's hands became badly blistered and had to be bandaged. After Flower left the Island, Tomás sent a card, the first of many, thanking him for the present of tobacco which he had sent and enquiring about his hands. The card was addressed to Flower at 10 Whitcomb Street, Pall Mall, London, and was written in Irish:

Ón mBlascaod Mór
A chara ardmheanmach, ba cheart dom teoirínnteacht a chur ar do thuairisc feasta, nár bhrea an síntiúis a chuirís chugam ón nDaingean, ná raibh do lámh choíche folamh, ba mhaith liom cuntas a fháil uait, má sé do thoil, é conas mar tánn tú' déanamh, an bhfuil rian an phiocóid ar do lámha fós? Mise agus ardmheas agam ortsa,
Tomás Ó Criomhthain

From the Great Blasket
My spirited friend, I will have to seek tidings of your condition from now on. Wasn't that a fine present you sent me from Dingle, may you never want. I should like to get an account from you as to how you are getting on. Is the mark of the pickaxe still on your hands? I am, with great regard for you,
Tomás Ó Criomhthain

Robin Flower married in the following year, 1911, and returned with his new wife to spend their honeymoon on the Island. The English scholar had married a young painter, Ida Mary Streeter, and she made a fine series of pen-and-ink drawings on the Island which adorn Flower's book about the Blaskets, *The Western Island* (Oxford, 1944).

In the first couple of years Flower and Tomás worked together for two or three sessions a day, Flower learning Irish, writing down short anecdotes and other material and Tomás teaching the young assistant from the British Museum as he had Marstrander.

Gradually Flower's Irish got to the stage where he began to record some of the wealth of Tomás's vast store of traditional lore. Flower's account of working with Tomás is an informative one and has always given me a real sense of the relationship between Tomás and Robin Flower when they sat together in the kitchen of the King's house or in Tomás's house at Bun an Bhaile.

And so, he sitting on one side of the table, rolling a savoury sprig of dillisk round and round in his mouth to lend a salt flavour to his speech, and I diligently writing on the other side, the picture of the Island's past grew from day to day under our hands. At times I would stop him as an unfamiliar word or strange twist of phrase struck across my ear, and he would courteously explain it, giving parallels from the local speech or illustrating with a little tale, budded off, as it were, from the larger unit.

The first world war put a temporary halt to Flower's visits to the Island, but Tomás and he continued to correspond. Flower returned after the war and began to work on *The Western Island*, a fine book by any standards, with insights into the life and history of the Island and its people. In time Robin Flower also brought his young family to the Island and they were sent to the Island school. Such was Flower's relationship with the Islanders that they fashioned an Irish form of his name and called him 'Bláithín' — little flower.

The work Flower accomplished on the Island enabled him to provide the world not only with his account of the community's culture in *The Western Island* but also a collection of Tomás Ó Criomhthain's stories and lore about the Blaskets, published when both were dead. *Seanchas ón Oileán Tiar* (Dublin, 1956), and it furnished him with material for his seminal study on Ireland and medieval Europe — *The Irish Tradition* (Oxford, 1947). Although the Island was well known within Ireland as an important source of Irish language material, it was Flower who put the Island on the literary map and brought its culture to a wider audience. He established, with some other English men, such as George Thomson, the Greek and Homeric scholar, and Kenneth Hurlstone Jackson, the Celtic scholar, a climate for the Island community in which it would be possible for the Islanders to write about their lives and the Island in their own language.

During the years of the second world war Flower worked at Aberystwyth in Wales, where he acted as custodian of the British Museum's manuscript collection removed out of London for safety. He became very seriously ill, suffering brain damage, and his memory gradually faded. His vast learning and knowledge were slowly erased. All that Robin Flower could remember in the final years were the days spent in the company of his friends on the Blasket Islands. He died in 1946. His favourite place on the Island was An Dún, at the back of the Island, the prehistoric fort site overlooking Carraig an Lóchair. He worked there frequently and it is from here that his ashes were scattered in the presence of the Island community.

Although it is quite clear that Flower had an enormous regard for Tomás Ó Criomhthain, I do not believe that he saw the potential in Tomás as a creative writer. Tomás benefited from the considerable personal contact he had with the English scholar and they both shared with each other their insights into literature, history and the very nature of man. Flower's Irish had, over the period up to the first world war, so improved as to enable him to speak with Tomás on a considerable intellectual level. Tomás drew on much of Robin Flower's knowledge of Irish and other literatures to enrich his own mind. Their correspondence enabled Tomás to write on topics other than folklore, which he had already been doing for Irish language publications. Tomás's ultimate contribution might have been confined to articles on folklore to various journals and his reputation might have rested solely on the publication of Robin Flower's books, including *Seanchas ón Oileán Tiar*, were it not for the arrival on the Island of a young graduate of Trinity College Dublin, Brian Ó Ceallaigh from Killarney.

The coming of Ó Ceallaigh was in time to bring into being the Ó Criomhthain autobiography — *An tOileánach* (*The Islandman*) and an equally important book, *Allagar na hInise* (*Island Cross-Talk*). Brian

Ó Ceallaigh, or Bryan Albert Kelly, was born in Killarney in 1889, the son of well-off parents in the hotel and drapery trade. The sons of the family went into law, the church and one became an air vice-marshall in the British Royal Air Force. Brian Ó Ceallaigh was educated with the Jesuits in Clongowes Wood College, County Kildare and at Blackrock College in Dublin before entering Trinity College Dublin at the age of eighteen. He graduated with a BA in 1911 and obtained his LLB in 1913.

Pádraig Ó Siochfhradha (An Seabhac), an Irish language teacher and scholar, was teaching Irish in the Killarney area at the time, and Ó Ceallaigh's mother asked him to help her son to learn Irish. Ó Siochfhradha recommended that Brian Ó Ceallaigh should go to a Gaeltacht area to learn the spoken language and gave him a letter of introduction to Tomás Ó Criomhthain in case he decided to go into the Island.

Brian Ó Ceallaigh came to the Great Blasket in April 1917 and he spent the rest of the year there. Tomás and Brian were to become close friends, and Brian was able to persuade Tomás to write an account of his life and what might be called an island sketchbook, giving short, lively and sharply written accounts of daily life on the Island.

During his time on the Island, Brian Ó Ceallaigh introduced Tomás to Pierre Loti's book, *Pecheur d'Islande (Iceland Fisherman)* (1886), and to some of Maxim Gorky's works. This was to show that the lives of ordinary people, fishermen and Russian peasants, could be the stuff of literature and, if so, why not the life of a Blasket Islander? Tomás had a certain sense of his own future as a writer. His efforts in learning to read and write in Irish when he was over forty is one piece of the evidence for that. The account in Tomás's autobiography of his encounter with the Island poet is another part of that evidence. Seán Ó Duinnshlé was an important person in Island life during the course of the nineteenth century and one of the Island's two poets during the period of Tomás's youth and early manhood.

I believe that Tomás Ó Criomhthain's genesis as a writer is set out by him in his account of this encounter with Ó Duinnshlé on a day when Tomás went cutting turf at the back of the Island. He had hardly started his work at the turf bank when Ó Duinnshlé turned up with a spade under his arm:

Ní dóigh liom go raibh file riamh le moladh chun aon obair shaothrach eile a chur chun cinn ach an fhilíocht amháin agus b'ín nua ag Seán é. Tá sórt deimhniú agam leis an abairt seo mar gach uair dá dtugaim féin faoi ranna a chur le chéile — ós minic déanta agam é — níor mhaith ar bhuíon ná ar mhachaire mé an fhaid a bhídís idir lámha agam.

I don't suppose that a poet could ever be lauded for hard work — only poetry, and that was true particularly of Seán. I can prove this, for every time I attempted to compose verse — and I have often it, I would need neither fish nor flesh while so engaged.

'Sea,' arsa an file liom, 'nach mór an obair duit a bheith ag baint mhóna a leithéid de lá chomh te leis,' á chaitheamh féin ar an dturtóg. 'Suigh, tamall,' ar seisean, 'tá an lá seo fada agus beidh fionnuar tráthnóna ann.'

Ní rabhas róbhuíoch dá chomhrá ach gur bhuail náire mé gan suí ina theannta. Rud eile, thuigeas mura mbeadh an file buíoch díom go ndéanfadh sé leibhéal orm ná beadh ar fónamh agus mé i mbéal mo thugtha amach san am seo. Shuíos ina theannta, agus gnó aige díom.

'Sea,' arsa an file liom, 'an chéad amhrán a dheineas riamh, b'fhéidir ná fuil sé agat. Is í an 'Chaora Odhar' an chéad cheann a dheineas, agus fáth maith agam lena déanamh maidir le holc.'

Cad deirir leis ná gur thosnaigh le gach focal a rá di agus é sínte siar ar shlat a dhroma, turtóg de mhínfhraoch thíos faoi agus teas agus brothall ó lonrach na gréine ag teacht anuas ón spéir fhíorghorm ghlan a bhí os ár gcionn an uair seo ag tabhairt teasaíochta don dtaobh os a chionn don fhile.

'Beidh an t-amhrán ar lár,' ar seisean, 'mura bpiocfair suas é. An bhfuil peann luaidhe i do phóca ná blúire de pháipéar?'

Mar an té ná bíonn an t-ádh ina bhóthar ar maidin agus Dia leis, níl sé i gcumas an pheacaigh bhoicht féin mórán a dhéanamh. Inseann an scéal seo sin, mar dhá ualach seanasail de mhóin níor thit le Tomás bocht an lá seo a raibh an saothar mór beartaithe aige le déanamh; agus bhí an lá seo ar na chéad laethanta riamh ar bhraitheas an saol ag teacht i mo choinne, mar is ea a bhí lá liom agus chúig lá i mo choinne as seo amach.

Is ea níorbh ar mhaithe leis an bhfile a fuaireas mo pheann luaidhe agus páipéar a bhí i mo phóca ach ar eagla go dtabharfadh sé aghaidh a gharbh-bhéil orm féin, agus chromas ar bhreacadh síos mar a ligeadh seisean as a bhéal. Ní sa teanga seo a bhíos ag scríobh mar ná rabhas oilte uirthi san am seo ach tuairim i mBéarla.

'Yes,' said the poet to me, 'isn't it extraordinary that you should be saving turf on a day as close as this,' throwing himself on the hummock. 'Sit a while,' he said, 'the day is long and it shall cool in the evening.'

I was hardly grateful for his conversation but not to sit with him would have been embarrassing. Another thing, I knew that if the poet was annoyed he would ridicule me, which would not help me as I was just about to go out on my own then. I sat with him, he certainly had something for me to do.

'Now,' said the poet, 'the first poem I ever made, perhaps you don't know it. The 'Caora Odhar' is the first poem I composed and I had good reason for its composition: anger.'

What do you suppose he did, but to start to recite every word of it, lying on the flat of his back, a hummock of fine heather under him and warmth and heat from the sunshine coming down from the clear blue sky now above us warming the uppermost part of the poet.

'The song will perish,' he said, 'unless you learn it. Have you a pencil in your pocket, or a piece of paper?'

He upon whom fortune does not shine in the morning nor God go with him, that pilgrim can achieve but little. This story is an example of that, for the unfortunate Tomás failed to save even what an old ass could carry in two loads of turf on that very day when he had planned to do so much work: and this day was one of the first days which I felt life going against me: from now on I had for every one good day, five bad days.

It wasn't to oblige the poet that I took out my pencil and paper which were in my pocket, but because I feared that he might abuse me, I began to take down what he recited. It was not in this language that I wrote because I didn't know how to then, but rather in a version using English characters.

There are several layers in the account. The poet was about sixty and Tomás a young man in his early twenties 'about to go out on his own'. It is a rather unusual encounter in Irish literature, where poetry is discussed and the 'apprentice' is required to transcribe a poem. There are authentic references from Irish tradition to the fear of being satirised by a poet: more originally, Tomás's allusions to his being 'wasted' after composition: the premonition — even with hindsight — of the difficulties which would attend Ó Criomhthain's decision to be a writer. Finally the remarkable feature of the story is that Tomás went to the hill with pencil and paper: a young man in his twenties around the year 1875!

Ó Criomhthain used the only important creative figure he had known from within his culture in the writing up of his genesis as a writer. Tomás doesn't find it necessary to explain why a young fisherman should go cutting turf with a pencil and paper in his pocket. How marvellous it would be to discover that piece of paper! The tone of this extract from the autobiography in its original Irish has a consistent echo of classical Irish literary tradition about it — it also has a Homeric tint.

When Brian Ó Ceallaigh left the Island on New Year's Eve, 1917, Tomás promised him that he would send him page by page an account of his life on the Island and that he would supply also a kind of daily account of Island life. Brian Ó Ceallaigh arranged to supply Tomás with sheets of bifoliate foolscap pages and gave him his Waterman's fountain pen. Tomás may have thought at the outset that Brian Ó Ceallaigh wanted this material so as to improve his own grasp of the language, but whatever about that, it became clear to the pair of them after a while that publication was necessary: Tomás and Brian kept up a correspondence throughout this venture, Tomás writing in Irish, Brian in English.

Brian Ó Ceallaigh became a national schools inspector in June 1918 and kept up the supply of paper, tobacco and other supplies to keep the task on course. Tomás wrote to Brian on a number of occasions on the Trinity College Historical Society writing paper which had obviously been supplied by Brian. What a speaker Tomás would have been at the 'Hist'!

Tomás began to write up the Island journal after Brian left the Island for the first time. Tomás was sixty-three years of age. The material accumulated so that by the time Tomás had finished the journal, later to be entitled *Allagar na hInise*, the manuscript consisted of 189 bifoliate pages and some single pages. This manuscript is now in the collection of Gaelic manuscripts in the National Library in Dublin (G 1022).

Some time at the end of 1923 Tomás had essentially finished the journal and commenced his autobiography and continued sending the autobiographical material to Brian until the middle of 1924 with occasional items from the journal as well.

At this stage, with a considerable amount of material from Tomás in manuscript form, the second book, the autobiography, was almost complete. This manuscript is also in the National Library (G 1020). Brian Ó Ceallaigh felt an obligation to the writer to have the material published. Brian, a solitary man with few friends, was becoming unhappy with his life as a schools inspector. He was not very strong and he may have been worried about his health. He decided to leave Ireland, but before he could do that he had to seek a publisher urgently or to interest somebody in Ó Criomhthain's work and have it published.

Ó Ceallaigh brought the manuscript to the Irish Texts Society in London, but in view of the work involved in preparing the text for the press, they felt unable to undertake the task. He even brought the material to Paris with him, but to no avail. Finally he went to see the Minister for Education, Eoin MacNeill, but the department did not at that time have a publications scheme in operation.

By this time Brian had become desperate. He had decided to leave the country and travel abroad to a warmer climate. He went to see Pádraig Ó Siochfhradha, the person who had first introduced him to the Blaskets, and urged him to look after the Ó Criomhthain work. Ó Siochfhradha, recognising the value of the material, agreed to undertake the task of editing the manuscripts and preparing them for publication.

Brian Ó Ceallaigh left Ireland never to return. Pádraig Ó Siochfhradha says that he left the country a 'lonely man'. We get one glimpse of Ó Ceallaigh in exile in Europe when he sent a letter to Ó Siochfhradha saying that he had met with Professor Séamas Ó Duilearga at a railway station in Berlin. Ó Duilearga, who founded the Irish Folklore Commission, told me that he was travelling from Berlin to Denmark with the Swedish folklorist Carl Von Sydow. Von Sydow had been in the Blaskets himself and had taken a series of important photographs of the Island community which are now to be seen as illustrations in the second edition of *Allagar na hInise*. As the train was leaving the platform, Ó Duilearga saw Ó Ceallaigh standing on the platform, and spoke to him from the window of the train. The conversation was about the Island. That, so far as we know, is the last contact Ó Ceallaigh had with Ireland.

Brian Ó Ceallaigh died in Split in Yugoslavia, and the municipal authorities gave me the details of the cause of his death at the state hospital. Ó Ceallaigh died of poliomyelitis on 28 December 1936. What brought him to Split we don't know — the climate perhaps. He was probably teaching there, but the details of his life after leaving Ireland are obscure. My wife and I had an opportunity to visit Split in 1986, and we found Brian's grave in the municipal cemetery of Lovrinac, just outside Split. The grave is identified by number, and a very dilapidated cross: no name appears on the grave itself.

Allagar na hInise appeared in 1928 and the autobiography *An tOileánach* came in 1929. It is doubtful if Brian Ó Ceallaigh saw either of the books to whose creation he had contributed so much.

Pádraig Ó Siochfhradha (better known by his pen-name, An Seabhach) edited the material and prepared the texts for publication. He got Tomás to fill in certain details of his life and to write the final and perhaps best known chapter of the autobiography. This last chapter is preserved amongst the Ó Siochfhradha papers in Dingle public library which also houses an important collection of material relating to the Corca Dhuibhne area collected by Ó Siochfhradha over a long period.

Unfortunately, Ó Siochfhradha, in editing the material, felt compelled to reduce both texts in length and cut some of the material for reasons of 'taste', in accordance with the fashion of the time. We still await definitive texts of both books and although second editions of each have been edited by Tomás Ó Criomhthain's grandson, Pádraig Ua Maoileoin, a novelist himself, these have also been abridged and portions of the texts omitted, apparently for 'literary reasons'.

Tomás Ó Criomhthain died just over two months after Brian Ó Ceallaigh's death, on 7 March 1937. He is buried in the little churchyard of Baile an Teampaill, Dún Chaoin: it snowed heavily the day Tomás died and the snow lay on the ground down to the cliff edge. The sea was very rough.

When the news of Brian Ó Ceallaigh's death filtered through to Ireland, Pádraig Ó Siochfhradha said in a talk given on Radio Éireann in March 1937 on the deaths of Brian and Tomás: 'Bhraitheas le teacht an scéil sin, go raibh tragóid uaigneach taréis a tharló — I felt with the coming of that news, that some lonely tragedy had happened.' I have been unable to come up with sufficient evidence to hazard a guess as to what Ó Siochfhradha had in mind.

Tomás was the first of the Island's writers and the most important. Tomás's own ambition to be a writer and the contact with the wider and more sympathetic knowledge and attitudes of English scholars in particular was of great benefit to him. The visiting scholars propped up the writing talent, and although the role of Brian Ó Ceallaigh was seminal to the whole endeavour, Flower, Marstrander and others were important strands in the literary fabric.

As to the Ó Criomhthain books themselves. An tOileánach (The Islandman) is autobiographical and covers the period of Tomás's life from his earliest childhood memories, just before 1860, to a time in the mid-1920s — a span of some seventy years. Allagar na hInise (Island Cross-Talk) is a sketchbook of daily life on the Island. The text teems with faces engrossed in conversation and observations, with Ó Criomhthain himself very much in the centre of each scene as the 'point of view', but giving us hints and background information. Tomás was probably not conscious, when Brian Ó Ceallaigh persuaded him at the end of 1917 to begin writing an account of his life and a daily journal, that a book, or books, would emerge.

It is important to put the whole undertaking in the context of its time. The use of the Irish language as a creative medium had virtually been 'retrieved' by a number of writers and scholars involved in the revival of the Irish language. The connection between what remained of the living language and the older literature had been broken: the living language was weakened and its native speakers were, in the main, illiterate. The Irish language did not have a continuous literary tradition. It had not had a standard literary norm for at least three hundred years. Therefore the early writers of the revival movement at the turn of the twentieth century had to overcome very great difficulties.

At the start of the nineteenth century anybody wanting to write in Irish had quite a task ahead of them, not the least of which was that the majority of the potential audience — those whose first language was Irish — could neither read nor write in their own language. The question of a literary norm had not been resolved, but the work in Irish by Patrick Pearse (1879-1916) and the novels of Father Peadar Ó Laoghaire (1839-1920) influenced the course of events.

Tomás Ó Criomhthain was living far away from the centre of this debate. His ability to both read and write in Irish was unusual. Priests, teachers and academics, yes, but a fisherman living in a remote island off a remote mainland? Tomás Ó Criomhthain had read two of Ó Laoghaire's novels: *Niamh*, with Carl Marstrander, and *Séadna*, with Brian Ó Ceallaigh. We know that Ó Ceallaigh introduced him to the work of Pierre Loti and Maxim Gorky in translation. These books formed part of Tomás Ó Criomhthain's library of books.

When Tomás, in 1918, began to write a picture of daily life on the Island, it was a voyage of discovery, with no chart except that of Ó Ceallaigh's encouragement. This book, *Allagar na hInise*, was written by Tomás for somebody who knew the Island well enough and was familiar with the characters: Tomás was engaged in a long-distance conversation with his friend Brian. On one occasion Tomás tells Brian that he has to close his journal now in order to meet the post deadline: the King, who was also the postman, was leaving in the morning.

Ní féidir liom a thuilleadh cuntais a thabhairt duit, a chara mo chroí. Beidh an Rí ag dul amach amáireach. Tá cuntas an lae inniu agam duit, ach ní féidir liom cuntas an lae amáirigh a thabhairt duit mar tá sé gan teacht ...	I can't give you a further account, my dear friend. The King will be going out tomorrow. I have today's account for you, but I can't give you the account for tomorrow for it hasn't come ...

The prose style of the *Allagar* is sharp and taut. Literary critics have drawn attention to the quality of 'prose poetry' which runs like a thread through the *Allagar* text:

Is lá geimhridh é agus a chuma air. Tá séideadh na gaoithe móire ag cur na farraige lastuas de gach a bhfuil sé ar a chumas é a dhéanamh. Níl aon radharc ar na stocáin mhara atá san fharraige le hanfa agus le cúrán bán ag gabháil lastuas díobh. Tá an féar a bhí glas inné feoite inniu. Tá craiceann na ndaoine féin ag athrú leis an ndrochaimsir. Tá caoirigh an chnoic séidthe óna n-áit lonnaithe agus iad d'iarraidh teacht isteach sna tithe chughainn. An breac a bhíodh ar feadh na bliana agus a bholg in airde le gréin i mbarr an uisce, tá sé curtha	It is a winter's day, and looks like it. The blast of the great wind is driving the waves over everything that it can reach. The rocks out to sea are hidden from sight by the squalls of white surf bursting over them. The grass that was green yesterday is withered today. Even the people's skins are changing in the bad weather. Sheep that have been blown out of their resting-places in the hills are trying to force their way into the houses. The fish that lay all summer sunning himself on the surface of the water, has vanished in the storm.

as amharc ag an síon. An ógbhean atá chomh píoctha ar feadh na bliana leis an eala ar an linn, nuair a thagann sí isteach le buicéad uisce bíonn an raca a bhíonn ina cúl sciobtha ag an ngaoth uaithi, a cuid gruaige ag teacht ina béal, ríoball ar a cuid éadaigh, leath an bhuicéid doirtithe aici agus í chomh gruama le duine a mbeadh ceal tobac air.

Na daoine aosta a raibh a gcnámha chomh bog chomh breá ar feadh na bliana le teas na gréine, tá cos ag crapadh faoi dhuine acu, fear eile agus a lámh ag bagairt air. Duine eile in imeall na tine agus súil á thabhairt air sara dtitfeadh sé isteach inti le codladh.

Is mó leigheas a bhíonn san aimsir bhreá agus is mó dochar a leanann an drochaimsir.

The young woman who was as spruce as the swan on the lake, when she comes in with a bucket of water, the comb has been snatched from the back of her head by the wind, her hair is straying into her mouth, there is mud on her clothes, the water is half spilt, and she is as cross as someone who is out of tobacco. Of the old people, whose bones had been so fine and soft in the warmth of the sun, one has a shrivelled leg, another complains of his arm, and another is dozing over the fire, and they are keeping an eye on him lest he fall into it.

There are many cures in fine weather and much harm in hard.

The *Allagar*, in this and in other examples, also echoes earlier Irish poetic tradition. It is doubtful if Tomás ever saw a swan on a lake, for instance, but his knowledge of songs from within the older tradition is evident here. This piece owes its pattern of a quickly projected range of short images to earlier nature poetry, and of course to Tomás's own epigrammatic style.

Before Tomás had finished his writing of the journal, Brian Ó Ceallaigh had persuaded him to start writing an account of his life. This was some time in 1922 and for a while the two works overlapped. Tomás was then sixty-seven. He was aware that each book demanded a different style and, as he says himself, he 'set the compass anew', drew out the corner-stones of the first book so that there would be no connection between the work which he had just finished and that which lay ahead of him. The *Allagar* text is an expansive narrative with a considerable amount of dialogue, crafted to provide further information and perhaps a 'colouring' on somebody's character. Ó Criomhthain was able to draw on his powers of recall when writing dialogue. A*n tOileánach*, on the other hand, is a somewhat stern book, although there are moments of lightheartedness, as we have seen when Tomás went courting into Inis Icíleáin. Tomás describes his fellow Islanders in a fairly detached way, noting many of their foibles, their drinking habits when in Dingle, and their physical courage when in danger, as was often the case when seal hunting and fishing in the heavy seas around the Island.

The printed versions of the two books and their published translations do not include everything Tomás wrote as there were substantial editorial cuts. A fuller assessment of Tomás Ó Criomhthain's writings can only be made when the complete and unabridged texts have been published.

Tomás Ó Criomhthain wrote one final book, a short commentary on the Blasket island placenames, *Dinnsheanchas na mBlascaodaí* (placename lore of the Blaskets) (1935), and his repertoire of Island lore which Robin Flower collected from him is published in *Seanchas ón Oileán Tiar* (lore from the western island) (1956).

My impression of the Blasket Island story is that once contact is made with the Island and its culture you can't escape from it, try as you might. It's like a long relay race in which the baton is passed from person to person to person. Touch the place once and it sticks to your hand forever.

CHAPTER 2

Muiris Ó Súilleabháin and George Thomson

Robin Flower sent other scholars to the Island. On the day on which the first elections in the Irish Free State under its newly established constitution were being held, 27 August 1923, a young classical scholar from Cambridge University, George Derwent Thomson, arrived in the town of Dingle on his way into the Island. Thomson knew modern Irish and this made the members of the recently formed Garda Síochána suspicious: an Irish-speaking Englishman! They thought perhaps he was an *agent provocateur*. George Thomson wanted to take Celtic for his degree at Cambridge, but the university did not offer an undergraduate course in that subject. Accordingly he read classics and was to distinguish himself in Greek. A meeting with Robin Flower brought him into contact with the Island. Thomson's visit was to have important consequences for a young Islander of about the same age, Muiris Ó Súilleabháin.

Muiris Ó Súilleabháin was born on 19 February 1904. He was the last of five children born to Seán Lís Ó Súilleabháin and Cáit Ní Ghuithín who had married in 1894. Cáit, Muiris's mother, was a daughter of Tomás Ó Criomhthain's sister, also Cáit. Muiris was just a year old when his mother died on the Island, far from a doctor or a hospital. The decision was taken to send Muiris to an orphanage in Dingle, where he was to be for six years. This was an unusual step for an Islander. There was an extended family: according to the 1901 census Muiris's mother and father and their three children were living in the household of Eoghan Ó Súilleabháin.

Muiris's grandfather, Eoghan, and Seán Lís did not get on together. By the census of 1911, Muiris's father, Seán Lís, is recorded as having his own house: a widower with a son and two daughters. Muiris returned to the Island later that year, but after the census was taken. The account of his return, in his autobiography *Fiche Blian ag Fás* (*Twenty Years a-Growing*), is the first account of the Island by an Islander who had spent some time away from it. Seán Lís brought his young son by pony and trap from Dingle to Dún Chaoin by Slea Head:

'Anois, a Mhuiris,' arsa m'athair, 'féach t'áit dhúchais' ag síneadh a mhéire siar ó thuaidh i dtreo oileáinín beag a bhí scriosta amach ón míntír. Níor labhras, do tháinig cnap im scornaigh nuair a chonac an tOileán.

'Now, Maurice, see your native place!' said my father, stretching out his hand north-west to a small island which had been torn out from the mainland. I could not speak: a lump came in my throat when I saw the Island.

'Ach,' arsa mise sa deireadh, 'conas is féidir leis an gcapall dul ansan isteach?'

'Ragham isteach le naomhóg,' arsa m'athair.

'Cad é an sórt rud an naomhóg?' arsa mise.

Níor chuireas a thuilleadh ceistiúcháin air ach mé ag síormhachnamh agus ag féachaint uaim isteach. Do chonac tithe beaga geala dlúite ina chéile i lár an Oileáin, cnoc mór fiain siar díreach gan aon tigh eile le feiscint ach amháin túr a bhí i mullach an chnoic agus an cnoc san bán le caoire thall is abhus. Níor thaithnigh an fhéachaint sin liom. Is dóigh liom, arsa mise im aigne féin, nach áit ar fónamh é ...

'But how can the horse get in there?' said I at last.

'We will go in with a *naomhóg*,' said my father.

'What sort of thing is a *naomhóg*?' said I.

I stopped questioning, and went on thinking and looking out. I saw little white houses huddled together in the middle of the Island, a great wild hill straight to the west with no more houses to be seen, only a tower on the peak of the hill and the hill-side white with sheep. I did not like the look of it. I think, said I to myself, it is not a good place ...

This is a realistic picture of the Island indicating its rather grim conditions. Muiris was, of course, able to view the Island in a different light to the other Island writers because of his early schooling in Dingle and his later life in Galway.

He went to school on the Island where the schoolmaster was Thomas Savage from north Kerry. The assistant teacher, Cáit Ní Mhainín, lodged in the house in the village. The population consisted of 160 people and the two-teacher school had a roll of just under seventy pupils. In 1911, when the young Muiris was going to school, the Island was in a healthy condition. Muiris's two sisters, Máire and Eilín, were also at school, as were two of Tomás Ó Criomhthain's sons, Muiris and Seán, and four of Peig Sayers's children including Mícheál (Maidhc File).

The Congested Districts Board was at work in the Island, with road improvements, the new pier and housing at Slinneán Bán at the back of the village. A foreman of the board, a Mayoman, was in digs in the house of the King. There was employment available with the board on the Island and a living to be made on the sea. This was a happy place for the young Ó Súilleabháin to be, and happy he was.

But Muiris had one small problem: as he had spent the previous six years in Dingle, he had no Irish! As the community's main language was Irish, and indeed many of them knew no English at all, Muiris quickly surmounted the language difficulty. He spent a lot of time in his grandfather's house. 'Daideo' (Grandad) Eoghan Ó Súilleabháin was in his seventies when Muiris got to know him. Eoghan was born sometime before 1850, a son of Mícheál Ó Súilleabháin who is remembered as a poet and became a Protestant in 1843. Eoghan married Lís Ní Ghuithín from Inis Icíleáin in 1864 and their eldest son, Seán Lís, was Muiris's father.

Eoghan was a remarkable storyteller and had a vast fund of knowledge about the Island lore, much of which Muiris acquired and indeed used in his autobiography and in other published material.

Muiris Ó Súilleabháin is remembered by the Islanders as having a great sense of fun and playing many a practical joke. He was a handsome young boy and several Island girls fell madly in love with him.

George Thomson was born in Dulwich, London, on 19 August 1903, and after education at Dulwich College he went to Cambridge where he won the classical tripos at King's College. He was to become a fellow of his college, and won the Craven scholarship which enabled him to teach at Trinity College Dublin and to write his first book, *Greek Lyric Metre* (Cambridge, 1927).

When Thomson first went into the Island his career, which was to be a distinguished one, lay before him. His friendship with Muiris Ó Súilleabháin and with Muiris's family, particularly with Muiris's grandfather, Daideo Eoghan Ó Súilleabháin, was what most interested him. Not only did Thomson have the companionship of a young man of his own age, but also a close contact with the Island's culture through Daideo, who was not only a gifted storyteller but an expert on Island lore.

At this stage in the life of the Island, the fishing had collapsed and emigration was draining the Island: all the young men and women were off to Springfield, Massachusetts. Muiris Ó Súilleabháin's two sisters and one of his brothers went to the United States. Another brother went to work in Dingle. Muiris would have gone also were it not for George Thomson, who persuaded him to avail of an opportunity created for young men from the Gaeltacht to join the Garda Síochána.

Muiris left the Island in March 1927 to become a member of the *gardaí* and went to the *garda* headquarters in the Phoenix Park in Dublin for training. George Thomson met him off the train and introduced him to Dublin city. It was Muiris's first visit to the capital and there is a marvellous account of his first impressions of the city in his autobiography *Fiche Blian ag Fás*. The train journey to Dublin was not without incident. Muiris took the wrong connection at Mallow and ended up in Cork. After completing his training he was posted to Inverin in the Conamara Gaeltacht.

Muiris Ó Súilleabháin was interested in writing and wanted to become a writer. George Thomson encouraged him in this venture, but the first results were disappointing. Even Muiris's account of the train journey to Dublin, via Cork, did not contain the humour to sustain the narrative. Muiris was a good storyteller, a facility which he had acquired from his grandfather, Daideo, but he could not, at that stage, re-create that talent in writing. It was the publication of Tomás Ó Criomhthain's *An tOileánach*, in 1929, which both acted as an incentive and provided an exemplar to Muiris.

George Thomson persuaded Muiris to take Tomás's book as a model and to write the events of his life up to the time he joined the *gardaí*. Muiris began to write *Fiche Blian ag Fás* in 1929 and to send it in sections as they were written to George Thomson.

Thomson, who by this stage had been elected a fellow of King's College, Cambridge, took up a position as a lecturer in Greek through Irish at University College, Galway, in 1931. The Greek lectureship was established to further the use of the Irish language as a teaching medium in Irish universities. There is a certain folklore concerning the Thomson appointment. It was very much the custom and practice in colleges of the National University to appoint clerics to many of the chairs and lectureships, particularly in the areas of education and the classics. When a George Derwent Thomson, a graduate of Cambridge, applied for the post, the authorities apparently felt that their clerical favourite would get the job because of the Irish language requirement: an Englishman with a sufficient capacity to teach through Irish was hardly likely. Clearly Thomson was academically qualified and so, during the course of the interview, the 'fail safe' test was applied. Could Mr Thomson give an example of his prowess to lecture in Irish? The candidate stood up and delivered himself of a lecture on Plato in Blasket Irish to the astonishment of the interview board. Accordingly, Thomson took up the position. The appointment was advantageous to the young Blasket *garda* in his ambition to become a writer, for now George Thomson was on the doorstep, so to speak, and they spent every Saturday in Galway discussing Muiris's book.

The manuscript, when complete, came to five hundred pages of closely written handwriting. Thomson felt that this was too long, and so, with Muiris's co-operation, he edited the text down to more manageable proportions. They submitted the text to the government publishing agency, An Gúm. An Gúm would only agree to publish the book if the references to Muiris and his friend Tomás Eoghain Bháin drinking pints at the Ventry races were removed. The authorities did not approve of reference to young boys from the Gaeltacht drinking. An Gúm also required an agreement that the book would not be published in translation in English. Thomson found these conditions unacceptable, and so he arranged for another publisher and subvented the publication financially himself.

Fiche Blian ag Fás was published in 1933 and was an instant success for the author. Thomson and Moya Llewelyn Davies published an English translation of the book in the same year and it achieved an extraordinary success in the English-speaking world. E.M. Forster wrote an introduction to the English version which puts *Fiche Blian ag Fás* in its literary context:

But it is worth saying 'This book is unique', lest he the reader forget what a very odd document he has got hold of. He is about to read an account of neolithic civilisation from the inside. Synge and others have described it from the outside, and very sympathetically, but I know of no other instance where it has itself become vocal and addressed modernity ... I know the author too. He is now in the Civic Guard in Connemara, and though he is pleased that his book should be translated, his main care is for the Irish original, because it will be read on the Blasket. They will appreciate it there more than we can, for whom the wit and poetry must be veiled. On the other hand, we are their superiors in astonishment. They cannot possibly be as much surprised as we are, for here is the egg of a sea-bird — lovely, perfect, and laid this very morning.

Muiris Ó Súilleabháin's autobiography, *Fiche Blian ag Fás*, is written about that part of his life up to his first posting as a *garda* in Conamara. It recounts the exploits of the young Islander and his friends in and out of the Great Blasket and the surrounding islands. The Ó Súilleabháin family is portrayed in some detail and in particular the grandfather, Daideo Eoghan. The book gives an account of life on the Island as seen by someone who, when writing it far away in Conamara, remembered all the good days but towards the latter part of the book touches on the persistent emigration which was then draining the Island of its young.

'Sea,' arsa Máire agus í ag ní na n-áraistí. Bhí an chuid eile againn suite timpeall na tine. D'iontaíomair go léir sall.

'Cad is ea?' arsa mo dhearthái Seán.

Lena linn sin, iontaíonn Máire isteach ar an mbord arís agus í ag leamhghairí. Tógann cupán don mbord agus iontaíonn orainn féin arís.

'Is é an sea é,' ar sise, 'go bhfuil an-mheá agam ar dhul go Meiriceá.'

'O, tá mhuise, a óinseach,' arsa Mícheál.

'Cad a chuir id cheann é sin?' arsa m'athair ag iontú uirthi agus lasadh ina ghnúis.

'Tá,' arsa Máire ag cromadh ar ghol, 'mar tá Cáit Pheig ag dul ann, agus níl aon ghnó agamsa anso nuair atá na cailíní go léir ag imeacht.'

'Dein do rogha rud,' arsa m'athair, 'níl éinne ag stop.'

'Ní raghaidh sí ann,' arsa Eilín, ag pusaíl ghoil, 'mar má théann, raghadsa leis ann.'

'Dhere, léimíg láithreach,' arsa m'athair agus a dhá láimh aige á chrothadh san aer, 'seo libh sall agus beidh an t-ór le fáil ar na sráideanna agaibh.

Lá arna mháireach, do scríobh Máire do dtín a haintín ag triall ar an gcostas.

'Well,' said Máire one day while she was washing the plates. The rest of us were sitting round the fire. We turned round.

'What is the "well"?' asked my brother Seán.

She turned back to the table again, smiling. Then taking up a cup she turned round again:

'The "well" is,' said she, 'that I have a great mind to go to America.'

'Oh, you have, musha, you foolish girl,' said Mícheál.

'What put that into your head?' said my father, his face flushing.

'I have indeed,' said Máire, beginning to cry, 'for Cáit Pheig is going and I have no need to stay here when all the girls are departing.'

'Do what you will,' said my father, 'no one is stopping you.'

'She won't go,' said Eilín, her lips trembling, 'or if she does I will go too.'

'Arra, fly away at once!' cried my father, waving his hands in the air, 'away with you over the sea and you will find the gold on the streets!'

Next day Máire wrote to her aunt for the passage money.

That short portrait of an emotional confrontation gives us an idea of the general quality of Ó Súilleabháin's dialogue writing and his ability to verbally characterise each of the participants. That extract also shows us the writer's sense of what was happening in the Island even when tinting the narrative with a slight nostalgia.

Fiche Blian ag Fás draws on the lore and history of the Island and here Muiris uses his grandfather's repertoire to considerable effect while uniting it with his own accounts of life on the Blaskets into a well-constructed story. It is a perceptive book and although written through the eyes of a young man, those very eyes focused well on the figures moving from house to house set against the 'great wild hill straight to the west'. *Fiche Blian ag Fás* has another element which is quite important: the eyes of the writer are able to look both outwards and inwards and to see the Island and its affairs in a way which was different from that of Ó Criomhthain and the other Island writers. A young man's book, it is of all the books the one most liked by the Islanders themselves, perhaps for its optimism.

The translation by George Thomson and Moya Llewelyn Davies established a reputation for the book, and perhaps established the translation as a book in itself. The English translation is, I think, better than the translation of *An tOileánach*. Thomson recognised the creative writer in Ó Súilleabháin and this is evident in his approach to the translation. I am sure Robin Flower held the Ó Criomhthain book in equal esteem, but as a history rather than a personal statement.

The success of *Fiche Blian ag Fás*, including its translations into English, French and German, encouraged Muiris to leave the *gardaí* in order to take up writing full time. When he decided to leave the *gardaí* he had also decided to marry. Five days after his resignation he married Cáit Ní Chatháin of Doire Fhatharta, Carraroe, in the Conamara Gaeltacht, and brought his wife back to the Island on their honeymoon.

Muiris Ó Súilleabháin had never really been satisfied as a policeman, and certainly he disliked the late night and early morning raids for illicit *poitín* stills. His life as a full-time writer was not to be a happy one either. He couldn't get a publisher for the second volume of his autobiography 'Fiche Blian faoi Bhláth' (twenty years a-flowering) This book remains unpublished. Muiris Ó Súilleabháin achieved some modest success as a contributor to newspapers and journals. He also wrote a number of plays, including some for radio, which were broadcast.

By this stage George Thomson had returned to England where he became Professor of Greek at Birmingham University. Muiris Ó Súilleabháin rejoined the *gardaí* in 1950; he drowned shortly afterwards while swimming at Salthill in Galway. Muiris and his wife Cáit had two children, Eoin and Máirín. With the problems involved in deriving an income from writing, things were difficult for the Ó Súilleabháin household. Muiris became very depressed: the second volume of his autobiography and another book, 'Domhnall Cháit Bhillí', were rejected by Dublin publishers.

Dylan Thomas came to the Island once in 1946 to research the background to a film script which he intended writing on *Twenty Years a-Growing*: Thomas walked to the back of the Island and had tea and brown bread in the village. He did not complete the screenplay, but part of it was published posthumously.

Muiris Ó Súilleabháin is buried far away from his beloved Island in a little seaside graveyard at Barr an Doire, near Carraroe in Conamara.

George Thomson left University College, Galway, following a disagreement with the college authorities about the extent and scope of an extension lectures scheme, particularly in the Gaeltacht areas. Thomson believed that the most important role the college could play in the Gaeltacht areas would be to bring university learning right into the villages and houses of the Gaeltacht and thereby introduce the people there to a body of learning which had been hidden from them. The college was not interested in Thomson's scheme and would not agree to support it or Thomson's future involvement with the scheme.

When Thomson left Galway he had published four books in Irish dealing with aspects of Greek scholarship. *Prométheus faoi Chuibhreach* is the most noteworthy; an introduction to Greek philosophy, *Tusnú na Feallsúnachta*, the most interesting, based on a series of lectures which he gave on the adult education courses in the Conamara Gaeltacht. Thomson inhabited the world of Greek and Homeric scholarship with ease. The bibliography of his published work is extensive by any standards.

Thomson never forgot the Blasket Islands or its people. They called him by the name which he gave himself in Irish — Seoirse Mac Tomáis. In his books on Homeric studies he mentions with gratitude the debt he owed to the Blasket culture for the insights which he got there into the Homeric question: how and in what manner were the Homeric poems written down for the first time? In his book *The Prehistoric Aegean* (1949) he explains the connection between the Blasket Islands culture and Homer:

Then I went to Ireland. The conversation of those ragged peasants, as soon as I learnt to follow it, electrified me. It was as though Homer had come alive. Its vitality was inexhaustible, yet it was rhythmical, alliterative, formal, artificial, always on the point of bursting into poetry. There is no need to describe it further, because it had all the qualities noted by Radlov in the conversation of the Kirghiz. One day it was announced that a woman in the village had given birth to a child. As my informant expressed it, *Tá sé tarraigthe aniar aici*, 'She has brought her load from the west'. I recognised the allusion, because often, when turf was scarce, I had seen the women come down from the hills bent double under packs of heather. What a fine image, I thought, what eloquence! Before the day was out I had heard the same expression from three or four different people. It was common property. After many similar experiences I realised that these gems falling from the lips of the people, so far from being novelties, were centuries old — they were what the language was made of: and as I became fluent in it they began to trip off my own tongue. Returning to Homer, I read him in a new light. He was a people's poet — aristocratic, no doubt, but living in an age in which class inequalities had not yet created a cultural cleavage between hut and castle.

Thomson became a Marxist and a member of the Communist party of Great Britain, and his book, *Marxism and Poetry* (1945), is an important insight into that ideology. His involvement with Marxism may have obscured, in Ireland at any event, his extraordinary contribution to Irish language and culture.

Thomson wrote an important essay on the Blasket island and its literature and culture. The first version he wrote in Irish — *An Blascaod Mar a Bhí* (1977) — and a second version in English — *The Blasket That Was* (1982). Just before he died, in 1987, George Thomson had completely revised the English version which he entitled 'Island Home'. This has yet to be published.   Some years ago, when making a documentary film on the Blasket Islands (*Oileán Eile* — *Another Island*, 1985), I had an opportunity of meeting George Thomson with his wife Katharine in their home in Birmingham. By this time he had retired from the chair of Greek at the university and he was working on a revision of the Muiris Ó Súilleabháin autobiography, which he completed before his death. He was working from the original manuscript which, when the revision was finished, he then sent to the National Library in Dublin: a final act of courtesy and friendship with Ireland. His eyesight was very poor at this point and he could only read with difficulty, and his voice was hardly audible so that he had to use a small microphone to speak to his visitors. We spoke about the Island and about Muiris Ó Súilleabháin. His mind raced over and back across the Island and conjured up the faces of his happy days there. He showed me a series of drawings which Muiris had made for a projected children's version of his book. They are in a naive style and important in their own right.

When I was leaving, and as the conversation was in Irish, we somehow drew on the expression often used by Island people on the occasion of a parting, 'Castar na daoine ar a chéile ach ní chastar na cnoic ná na sléibhte — The people meet but not the hills nor the mountains.' George Thomson told me that the first time he had heard this expression was on the occasion of his departure from the Island. Muiris Ó Súilleabháin's grandfather, Daideo, was the person who uttered it. The last time Thomson heard it was when he was leaving a small Greek island when a traditional singer bade him farewell in Greek.

If Robin Flower had been fortunate in his contact and friendship with Tomás Ó Criomhthain, then George Thomson was equally fortunate in his friendship with Muiris Ó Súilleabháin. In a sense, his contact with the Ó Súilleabháin family brought him right into the centre of the Island's literary and storytelling tradition.

CHAPTER 3

Peig Sayers
and Other Writers

Tomás Sayers and Peig Ní Bhrosnacháin were married in 1851. They buried nine of their children so that in the end only four survived — Seán, Pádraig, Máire and Peig. They had been over twenty years married when Peig was born and her mother was in poor health. Peig tells us in her autobiography that her mother felt that the ill luck which had attended the family might cease if they were to move from Ventry, where they had lived, and an opportunity arose to acquire a small holding in Baile Viocáire, Dún Chaoin, from a family bound for America. The Sayers family moved to Dún Chaoin in 1872 and Peig was born in the following March, to the delight of her mother. She was baptised in Ballyferriter on 29 March 1873.

Peig attended the little national school at Baile Viocáire which is still serving the needs of the Irish-speaking community to this day. She went to school when she was six years of age, in 1879, and stayed at school until 1887, when she was fourteen years of age. Máire, her elder sister, ran the household because of their mother's poor health, and the economic circumstances of the family were such that her brother Pádraig had to go into service in Killarney from the age of twelve. Peig herself was to follow that path quite soon both because of financial necessity and because of the tensions which had developed in the house between her brother Seán's wife, Cáit, and Tomás, Peig's father, and indeed Peig herself. There was row after row, and eventually Peig herself got caught up in rows. Peig may have been jealous of her sister-in-law as she had been very close to her brother Seán. He was a good deal older than she and was like a father to her. Peig was the pet of the house, and she resented the intrusion of Cáit into their life. She spent four years in service in Dingle and returned to Baile Viocáire when her health began to cause her concern.

Peig had decided, like many a young person from the area, to go to America. Her school-friend, Cáit Jim, who lived just across the river from her in Baile Viocáire, had promised to send Peig some money for the fare when she got a job in America. To augment that, Peig decided to go into service again, this time with a big farmer at Cnoc an Bhróigín to the east of Dingle. The work here was slavery and Peig frequently went underfed as the farmer and his wife were misers.

When Peig returned once again to Baile Viocáire it was to bury her brother Pádraig's wife. This was not the only bad news awaiting her: she also got a letter from her friend Cáit Jim to explain that as she had damaged her hand and therefore could not work, it was not possible to forward Peig the fare to America. The Sayers family could not sustain a young woman without an income. Seán, Peig's brother, arranged a 'match' with a Blasket Islander. There was nothing unusual about these arranged marriages at the time: far from it. Furthermore a young girl marrying into the Island did not have to provide a dowry. Peig says about the match:

Níor mhór an mhoill an cleamhnas úd a dhéanamh, fóraoir!
Ní raibh aoinní ann ach 'Téanam' agus 'Táim sásta'.
Tháinig m'athair chugham anall.
'Tóg suas do cheann,' ar seiseann, 'an raghaidh tú 'on Oileán?'

That match didn't take much time, alas!
There was nothing but 'Come' and 'I'm happy'.
My father came over to me.
'Lift up your head,' said he, 'will you go into the Island?'

Peig Sayers and her Island partner, Pádraig Ó Guithín, were married on 13 February 1892. Peig was just short of nineteen years. Her husband Pádraig (Peatsaí Flint) was thirty years old. Peig went with her husband to live with his parents and an extended family at Bun an Bhaile — bottom of the village. The circumstances for a young bride were difficult, although perhaps not that different from the Baile Viocáire household. Peig married into a large household who lived in a very small house. Even in the 1901 census, when she had had three children, she was still living with her in-laws. In that census Peig is recorded as living with her husband, mother- and father-in-law, three children and two brothers-in-law. By the census of 1911 the situation had not improved. Peig then had six children.

I don't think that Pádraig Ó Guithín (Peatsaí Flint) was ever very strong and the housing conditions in which they lived on the Island must have contributed to his poor health. It was to be almost twenty years before Peig and her husband were to get a house of their own. Peatsaí Flint had worked on the construction of the new Congested Districts Board's houses at Slinneán Bán and they managed to get one of them.

Like her mother before her, Peig saw some of her children to the grave and others to America. Of her ten children, six survived: Cáit, Eibhlín, Muiris, Pádraig, Mícheál and Tomás. Tomás died when he fell down a cliff face. Pádraig went to America to be followed by Cáit. Peatsaí, her husband, who was by now an invalid, died. Next Muiris went to America and eventually Eibhlín (Neilí) and for a time Peig's poet son Mícheál (Maidhc File). Neilí is the only surviving member of Peig's family: she lives in Boston. Despite all this turmoil and difficulty, Peig, as is very evident from her autobiography, continued to be a very outgoing person. Her great interest in the comings and goings of her surroundings, lore, her vast repertoire of folktales and her faith sustained her and kept her not only in charge of the situation but allowed her to enter into the third phase of her life and to achieve recognition as one of the last of the great storytellers of the Gaelic tradition.

As contact with the outside world opened up for Tomás Ó Criomhthain with the visits of scholars, so also did it open up for Peig Sayers. Robin Flower recognised Peig's prowess as a storyteller and in time introduced Peig to his students and friends and referred to her frequently during the course of lectures on aspects of the Blasket culture.

One of those scholars whom Flower introduced to the Island was Kenneth Jackson, a young Englishman. Flower urged Jackson to visit Peig and to begin collecting her stories. Jackson first came to the Island in 1932 and he and Peig became very close friends. Jackson learned much of his spoken Irish from her and began the process of collecting part of her very rich repertoire of folktales. These he published in 1938 under the title *Scéalta ón mBlascaod* (stories from the Blasket). It is a rich collection of international tales, romantic tales and adventures, tales of the supernatural, moral tales and tales of saints and miracles.

Kenneth Hurlstone Jackson was born in 1909 and read classics at Cambridge. He was Professor of Celtic Languages, Literatures, History and Antiquities at Edinburgh University from 1950 to 1979. He is one of the leading Celtic scholars and his published work ranges over studies in all the Celtic languages of these islands, Breton, Scots Gaelic in Canada and studies in folklore and the folktale tradition.

Jackson remembers that Peig was rather a tall woman, with the most beautiful eyes, violet in colour and triangular in shape. 'It was easy to see,' Jackson told me, 'that Peig had been a beauty when she was young.' When Jackson met Peig for the first time, she was a grey-haired woman entering her sixties. Professor Jackson said that Peig was a strong character, very unlike the frontispiece photograph in the first edition of her autobiography. This photograph is still carried on the cover of the schools edition of her book, *Peig*. She had, according to Jackson, a tremendous sense of humour: 'She was shrewd and could show a sharp tongue when she wanted to.' Indeed, all that I have heard about Peig from those who knew her confirms Kenneth Jackson's description.

The Blaskets in the 1930s, during the summer months at any rate, were a focal point for those learning Irish. By this stage the writings of Tomás Ó Criomhthain and Muiris Ó Súilleabháin had been published and widely acclaimed. Young men and women came in their droves to the Island to study the language. During this period Peig came to know two women visitors, one a scholar, the other a student — Máire Ní Chinnéide and Léan Ní Chonnalláin. They urged Peig to record her life's story and eventually her son Mícheál — Maidhc File — wrote down a version of Peig's life from her speech. Peig could neither read nor write in Irish.

Like the rest of his family, Mícheál had gone to Boston to make his fortune, but his health and nerve broke and he returned to the Island. Mícheál had always been interested in writing. He wrote some poetry and was known affectionately by the Islanders as 'An File' (the poet). Maidhc File was one of those Islanders who, being aware of the relationship between Brian Ó Ceallaigh and Tomás Ó Criomhthain, wrote a diary account for Ó Ceallaigh of life on the Island for the year 1923 and five months of 1924. Interestingly, Muiris Ó Súilleabháin's sister, Eibhlín, was another 'writer' who kept a diary account for Brian Ó Ceallaigh. Both manuscripts are now in the National Library of Ireland in Dublin.

Peig, the autobiography orally 'written' by Peig and 'transcribed' by her son, was published by An Seabhac in a version edited by Máire Ní Chinnéide in 1936. The book has been a prescribed text for the leaving certificate (final schools examination) and as a result many thousands of Irish students over the years have come to know of Peig. Course texts often tend to suffer at the hands of a poor syllabus, teachers and students. *Peig* is an important book, but its very authorship alone makes it a complex text for second-level students.

The Peig autobiography covers an extensive canvas, from the period of early childhood, to her marriage in the Island, to the return of Mícheál from America and then up to about 1934. It is difficult to decipher from the text who 'wrote' what. Peig, to judge from those who knew her and those who tapped the vast supply of folklore which she possessed, used a vigorous form of language which was very rich and colloquial, but had strands of formality where required. She was not given to being a 'holy Mary' although she had an exceptional faith in God and in the Blessed Virgin.

Mícheál, at this stage of his life, was given to great bouts of gloominess: his sense of fun had gone after his experience in America. He was also a firm believer in fairies and in the supernatural. Mícheál, being a writer, also took an interest in language and in the written work of other writers.

One of the most moving accounts in the autobiography is that of the death in 1920 of Peig's son, Tomás. This was the year in which there was no turf on the Island and the Islanders had to collect every form of growth which might provide fuel for their meagre fires. It is breakfast time on a Friday in April 1920. Peig and one of her sons, Tomás, are up earlier than the others. Peig tells Tomás that his brother Pádraig is thinking of going to America but that she would prefer if he waited another year as the rest of the family were just that bit too young to handle a *naomhóg*. Tomás thinks that Pádraig is quite right to go, and asks if she believes that he couldn't look after her in his brother's stead. Tomás decides not to go to the hill that day. Peig agrees as she thinks the furze is too wet. That was the last time she saw Tomás alive: he fell off a cliff face trying to get a tuft of heather for the fire.

... sceon agus uafás i gcroí gach aon duine. Ba rud é nár thit amach riamh roimhe sin san Oileán, is mhéadaigh sin an t-uafás ar gach aon duine. Ach i mo thaobhsa de, ní féidir le peann scríobh ar cad a d'fhulaingíos is ar ar ghabhas tríd. Bhí sé sin marbh, bhí a athair le bliain roimhe sin ag coimeád na leapa, is nuair a chuala sé an tuairisc, an liú uafásach bróin a chuir sé as beidh i mo chroí go deo. Dá mb'fhéidir leis an leaba a fhágaint, bheadh sé go maith, dar leis, ach bhí sin ag teip air.

B'shin í an fhadhb — conas a d'imeoinn uaidh agus é fhágaint ansin i gcróilí an bháis? Bhí Tomás ag Dia, ach bhí sé sin beo fós, agus thuigeas i m'aigne gur bheart in aghaidh Dé dom an tigh fhágaint agus gan aon duine chun féachaint ina dhiaidh. Thug Dia an méid sin meabhrach dom, moladh go geo leis! gur fhanas chun lámhaíocht a thabhairt leis.

B'éigin do dhá naomhóg agus ochtar fear dul chun an corp a thabhairt leo. Is orthu a bhí an t-ionadh nuair a chuadar mar a raibh sé ... é chomh cóirithe is chomh socair is dá mbeadh dáréag ban ina fheighil ...

Nuair a tugadh go dtí an tigh é, bhí an chuid eile den chlainn scanraithe ... i dtaobh an fhir bhreoite b'athair dóibh, níorbh fhios dom cén nóimeat a thitfeadh an t-anam as ... le méid an scanradh a bhí ar na comharsana, bhí scáth orthu teacht i mo ghaire, ach aon bheirt amháin, Seán Eoghain agus Máire Ní Scannláin ... Bhí obair chruaidh le déanamh, ach cé dhéanfadh í? B'shin í an fhadhb! Ní raibh ionam ach máthair agus beart róchrua dom ba ea é! Mise nár mhaith liom gearradh a fheiscint, bhí orm fáscadh go dtí mo bhuachaill breá óg a ní agus a ghlanadh, agus cóir mhairbh a thabhairt dó! ...

... fear and awe seized the heart of everyone, for this was something that had never happened before on the Island and this multiplied everybody's terror. As far as I was concerned, no pen can describe what I suffered and endured. He was dead, his father had for the previous year been bedbound, and when he heard the news, the awful cry of sorrow which he uttered will remain in my heart for ever. If he could only leave the bed, he'd be fine, he thought, but he failed.

This was the problem, how could I go away from him and leave him there on his deathbed? Tomás was with God, but he was alive yet, and I knew in my mind that it would be an act against God to leave the house without somebody to take care of him. God gave me that much intelligence, praise to him always, that I stayed to mind him.

Two *naomhóga* and eight men had to bring the body with them. They were taken aback when they went to where he was ... quite well laid out and at rest as if twelve women had attended to him ...

When he was brought to the house, the rest of the family were terrified ... as to their sick father, I didn't know at what minute he might die ... with the neighbours so terribly frightened, they were nervous to come near me, but for two, Seán Eoghain and Máire Ní Scannláin ... There was a great deal to be done, but who would do it? That was the problem! I was only a mother and that task was beyond me! Me who wouldn't look at a cut, I had to compel myself to wash my fine young boy and lay him out in death ...

It is a fine piece of writing but it draws heavily on the great speech quality which Peig so evidently had.

Peig was followed in 1939 by a second volume of Peig's memoirs and stories, *Machtnamh Sean-Mhná* (*An Old Woman's Reflections*). The English translation of *Peig* was published in 1974: the translator was the writer Bryan MacMahon and Séamus Ennis translated the second of the Peig volumes in 1962.

Mícheál Ó Gaoithín published a third volume on Peig giving further accounts of her life. The material is rather thinly spread in the second and third volumes of the trilogy and their publication owes much more to the support which the publishers hoped to get from readers interested in the language revival than to any profound literary cause.

Maidhc File wrote a short but interesting autobiography himself. Is Trua ná Fanann an Óige (A Pity Youth does not Last), which was published in 1953 and in translation in 1982. An File's most important work is perhaps contained in a slim volume of poetry which was published in 1968: Coinnle Corra (bluebells) is a volume of poetry which must be included on the shelf of quality verse in Irish. It stands alone, and when it was published it caught those who knew Mícheál Ó Gaoithín by surprise. Now we had a clear view of a writer whose message was for the future. The poet took up painting and drawing with the encouragement of the artist Maria Simonds-Gooding and his emerging talent is an indication of what might have been.

Peig and her poet son Maidhc moved out of the Island in 1942 and they went to live at Baile Viocáire, Dún Chaoin. Her eyesight gradually failed and she became blind. Peig spent her last years in Dingle hospital, holding court with a stream of visitors and attended by her son. Peig Sayers died on 8 December 1958. Mícheál Ó Gaoithín lived out the rest of his days in the house at Baile Viocáire and died in 1974. Mother and son are buried in the new graveyard at Dún Chaoin looking out over the Island.

Whatever about Peig's reputation in the literary and outside world, her role within the village on the Island was an important one. Her prowess as a storyteller packed her kitchen at Slinneán Bán with an audience of young and old as they listened to her stories. Peig's house was also used by the young people of the Island to hold a céilí. After the dancing and singing, the young people, including Muiris Ó Súilleabháin, his cousin Maidhc File and others would wander down through the village, young men and women hand-in-hand to another day on the Island.

If one has the impression at this stage that every inhabitant on the Island was busily writing to the exclusion of every other form of activity, there is a certain truth in that. Dublin Opinion, the 'national humorous magazine of Ireland', carried a cartoon on its cover in the June edition of 1933 showing an island with every conceivable form of writing activity in progress: manuscripts and typewriters strewn all over the island and the islanders themselves engaged in literary pursuits. The cartoon is entitled 'The Literary Wave Hits the Islands'.

The writing tradition didn't cease with Ó Criomhthain, Ó Súilleabháin and Peig Sayers. As we have seen, Peig's son Mícheál (An File) Ó Gaoithín was a writer and poet. Seán Ó Criomhthain (1898-1975), son of Tomás, wrote an important book on the dispersal of the Island community and on his life and that of his young family at the northern end of the parish: Lá dár Saol (a day in our life), was published in 1969. Eibhlís Ní Shúilleabháin (1911-71), wife of Seán Ó Criomhthain, wrote a series of letters in English to George Chambers over a twenty-year period about her life on the Island and afterwards on the mainland. Chambers visited the Island in 1931 and 1938. A selection of these letters was published in 1978 — *Letters from the Great Blasket*.

Pádraig Ua Maoileoin (1913-), a grandson of Tomás Ó Criomhthain, was born on the mainland. He has written a series of novels of which *Bríde Bhán* (fair Bríd) (1968) and *Ó Thuaidh!* (action!) (1983) deal with aspects of the Gaeltacht culture of Corca Dhuibhne in which the Blaskets now play a ghostly part. He also wrote a series of essays broadcast on Raidió na Gaeltachta on the Corca Dhuibhne Gaeltacht, including his recollections of his grandfather, Tomás Ó Criomhthain. The radio series and the subsequent book — *Na hÁird ó Thuaidh* (the highlands to the north) (1960) — helped to resuscitate an interest in the Corca Dhuibhne Gaeltacht and in the Blaskets. Ua Maoileoin also edited versions of *An tOileánach* (1973) and *Allagar na hInise* (1977).

Seán Sheáin Í Chearnaigh (1912-), whose maternal grandmother, Máire, was a sister of Tomás Ó Criomhthain, was the last postmaster on the Island and he wrote two books on Island life — *An tOileán a Tréigeadh* (the island which was evacuated) (1974) and *Iarbhlascaodach ina Dheoraí* (a former Blasketman as an exile) (1978).

Máire Ní Ghuithín (1909-) was the granddaughter of An Rí and her mother Máire was the 'little hostess' in Synge's account of the Island. She has written two books giving an account of aspects of Island life from a woman's point of view — *An tOileán a Bhí* (the island that was) (1978) and *Bean an Oileáin* (woman of the island) (1986).

It was George Thomson who called that collection of books 'the Blasket Island library': and so it is. The 'library' is probably unique in the history of literature. It was written by the Islanders themselves from within their own culture, a collective portrait of their community just before its destruction. When the Island community sensed that their world was coming to an end they wrote it all down. Some did it well and their writings now form part of a universal literature and Tomás Ó Criomhthain, Muiris Ó Súilleabháin and Peig Sayers will live as long as books are read. The rest is a small footnote for Irish readers and those interested in island cultures.

But the Blasket library might never have been written were it not for the fortunate contact which the Islanders' culture made with a number of sensitive scholars from England and Norway and a schools inspector from Killarney. When Brian Ó Ceallaigh was encouraging Tomás Ó Criomhthain to write he told him that he ought not follow the poet Seán Ó Duinnshlé's example, but rather to leave a written account of his life and that of the Island community:

Chun go mbeinn beo is mé marbh

So that I would be alive while dead

THE BLASKETS

A KERRY ISLAND LIBRARY

A Genealogical Chart illustrating the relationship betwe

BLASKET ISLAND WRITERS

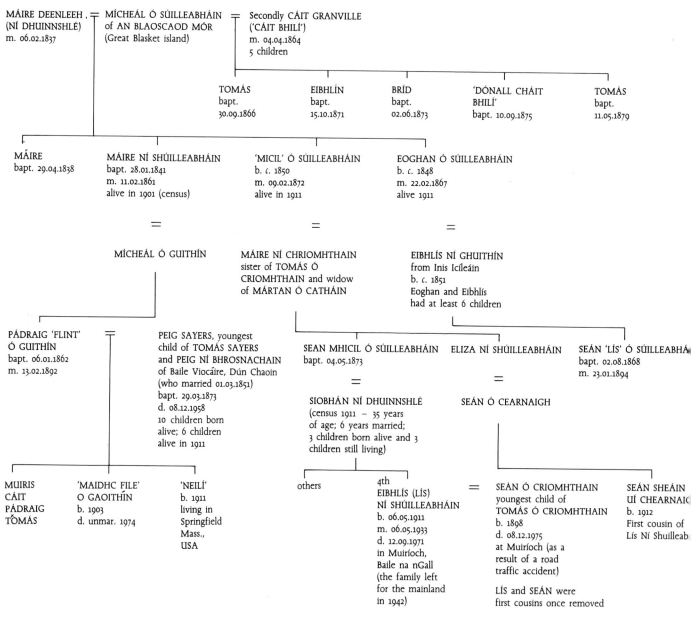

MÁIRE DEENLEEH , = MÍCHEÁL Ó SÚILLEABHÁIN = Secondly CÁIT GRANVILLE
(NÍ DHUINNSHLÉ)   of AN BLAOSCAOD MÓR   ('CÁIT BHILÍ')
m. 06.02.1837   (Great Blasket island)   m. 04.04.1864
                                                 5 children

TOMÁS   EIBHLÍN   BRÍD   'DÓNALL CHÁIT   TOMÁS
bapt.   bapt.   bapt.   BHILÍ'   bapt.
30.09.1866   15.10.1871   02.06.1873   bapt. 10.09.1875   11.05.1879

MÁIRE   MÁIRE NÍ SHÚILLEABHÁIN   'MICIL' Ó SÚILLEABHÁIN   EOGHAN Ó SÚILLEABHÁIN
bapt. 29.04.1838 bapt. 28.01.1841   b. c. 1850   b. c. 1848
                 m. 11.02.1861   m. 09.02.1872   m. 22.02.1867
                 alive in 1901 (census) alive in 1911   alive 1911

                 =   =   =

MÍCHEÁL Ó GUITHÍN   MÁIRE NÍ CHRIOMHTHAIN   EIBHLÍS NÍ GHUITHÍN
                         sister of TOMÁS Ó   from Inis Icíleáin
                         CRIOMHTHAIN and widow   b. c. 1851
                         of MÁRTAN Ó CATHÁIN   Eoghan and Eibhlís
                                                    had at least 6 children

PÁDRAIG 'FLINT' = PEIG SAYERS, youngest   SEAN MHICIL Ó SÚILLEABHÁIN   ELIZA NÍ SHÚILLEABHÁIN   SEÁN 'LÍS' Ó SÚILLEABHÁ
Ó GUITHÍN   child of TOMÁS SAYERS   bapt. 04.05.1873   bapt. 02.08.1868
bapt. 06.01.1862 and PEIG NÍ BHROSNACHAIN   m. 23.01.1894
m. 13.02.1892   of Baile Viocáire, Dún Chaoin   =   =
                 (who married 01.03.1851)
                 bapt. 29.03.1873   SIOBHÁN NÍ DHUINNSHLÉ   SEÁN Ó CEARNAIGH
                 d. 08.12.1958   (census 1911 – 35 years
                 10 children born   of age; 6 years married;
                 alive; 6 children   3 children born alive and 3
                 alive in 1911   children still living)

MUIRIS   'MAIDHC FILE'   'NEILÍ'   others   4th   =   SEÁN Ó CRIOMHTHAIN   SEÁN SHEÁIN
CÁIT   O GAOITHÍN   b. 1911   EIBHLÍS (LÍS)   youngest child of   UÍ CHEARNAIG
PÁDRAIG   b. 1903   living in   NÍ SHÚILLEABHÁIN   TOMÁS Ó CRIOMHTHAIN   b. 1912
TÓMÁS   d. unmar. 1974 Springfield   b. 06.05.1911   b. 1898   First cousin of
                           Mass.,   m. 06.05.1933   d. 08.12.1975   Lís Ní Shuilleab
                           USA   d. 12.09.1971   at Muiríoch (as a
                                                    in Muiríoch,   result of a road
                                                    Baile na nGall   traffic accident)
                                                    (the family left
                                                    for the mainland   LÍS and SEÁN were
                                                    in 1942)   first cousins once removed

Ó CRIOMHTHAIN, Ó SÚILLEABHÁIN and Ó GUITHÍN (Peig Sayers) families.

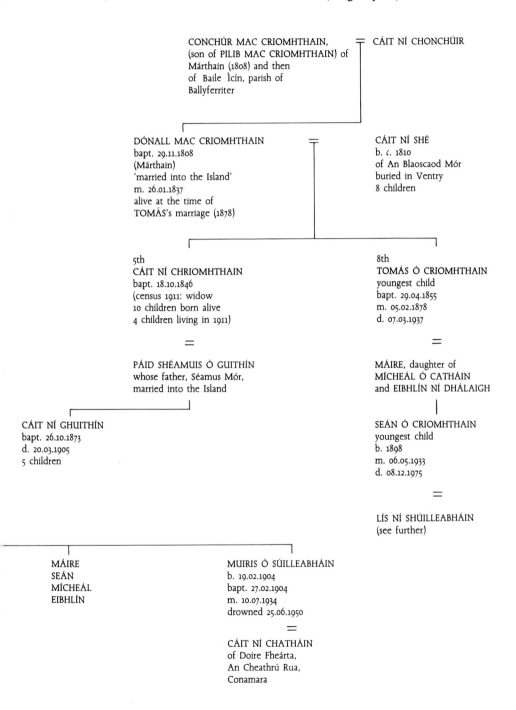

CONCHÚR MAC CRIOMHTHAIN,
(son of PILIB MAC CRIOMHTHAIN) of
Márthain (1808) and then
of Baile Ícín, parish of
Ballyferriter

⊤ CÁIT NÍ CHONCHÚIR

DÓNALL MAC CRIOMHTHAIN
bapt. 29.11.1808
(Márthain)
'married into the Island'
m. 26.01.1837
alive at the time of
TOMÁS's marriage (1878)

=

CÁIT NÍ SHÉ
b. c. 1810
of An Blaoscaod Mór
buried in Ventry
8 children

5th
CÁIT NÍ CHRIOMHTHAIN
bapt. 18.10.1846
(census 1911: widow
10 children born alive
4 children living in 1911)

=

PÁID SHÉAMUIS Ó GUITHÍN
whose father, Séamus Mór,
married into the Island

8th
TOMÁS Ó CRIOMHTHAIN
youngest child
bapt. 29.04.1855
m. 05.02.1878
d. 07.03.1937

=

MÁIRE, daughter of
MÍCHEÁL Ó CATHÁIN
and EIBHLÍN NÍ DHÁLAIGH

CÁIT NÍ GHUITHÍN
bapt. 26.10.1873
d. 20.03.1905
5 children

SEÁN Ó CRIOMHTHAIN
youngest child
b. 1898
m. 06.05.1933
d. 08.12.1975

=

LÍS NÍ SHÚILLEABHÁIN
(see further)

MÁIRE
SEÁN
MÍCHEÁL
EIBHLÍN

MUIRIS Ó SÚILLEABHÁIN
b. 19.02.1904
bapt. 27.02.1904
m. 10.07.1934
drowned 25.06.1950

=

CÁIT NÍ CHATHÁIN
of Doire Fheárta,
An Cheathrú Rua,
Conamara

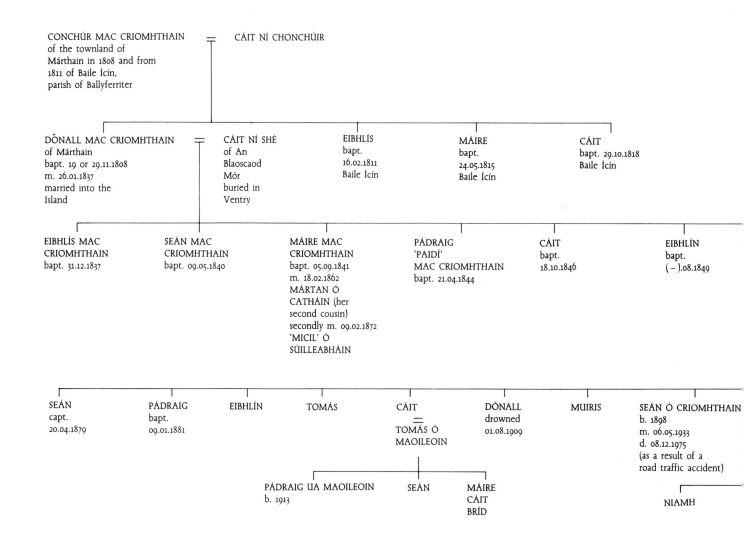

CONCHÚR MAC CRIOMHTHAIN of the townland of Márthain in 1808 and from 1811 of Baile Ícín, parish of Ballyferriter = CÁIT NÍ CHONCHÚIR

DÓNALL MAC CRIOMHTHAIN of Márthain bapt. 19 or 29.11.1808 m. 26.01.1837 married into the Island = CÁIT NÍ SHÉ of An Blaoscaod Mór buried in Ventry

EIBHLÍS bapt. 16.02.1811 Baile Ícín

MÁIRE bapt. 24.05.1815 Baile Ícín

CÁIT bapt. 29.10.1818 Baile Ícín

EIBHLÍS MAC CRIOMHTHAIN bapt. 31.12.1837

SEÁN MAC CRIOMHTHAIN bapt. 09.05.1840

MÁIRE MAC CRIOMHTHAIN bapt. 05.09.1841 m. 18.02.1862 MÁRTAN Ó CATHÁIN (her second cousin) secondly m. 09.02.1872 'MICIL' Ó SÚILLEABHÁIN

PÁDRAIG 'PAIDÍ' MAC CRIOMHTHAIN bapt. 21.04.1844

CÁIT bapt. 18.10.1846

EIBHLÍN bapt. (–).08.1849

SEÁN capt. 20.04.1879

PÁDRAIG bapt. 09.01.1881

EIBHLÍN

TOMÁS

CÁIT = TOMÁS Ó MAOILEOIN

DÓNALL drowned 01.08.1909

MUIRIS

SEÁN Ó CRIOMHTHAIN b. 1898 m. 06.05.1933 d. 08.12.1975 (as a result of a road traffic accident)

PÁDRAIG UA MAOILEOIN b. 1913

SEÁN

MÁIRE CÁIT BRÍD

NIAMH

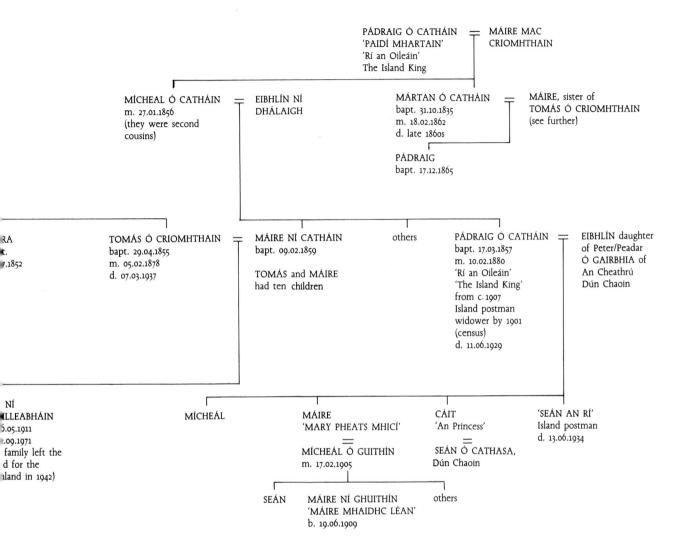

PÁDRAIG Ó CATHÁIN
'PAIDÍ MHARTAIN'
'Rí an Oileáin'
The Island King
= MÁIRE MAC CRIOMHTHAIN

MÍCHEAL Ó CATHÁIN
m. 27.01.1856
(they were second cousins)
= EIBHLÍN NÍ DHÁLAIGH

MÁRTAN Ó CATHÁIN
bapt. 31.10.1835
m. 18.02.1862
d. late 1860s
= MÁIRE, sister of TOMÁS Ó CRIOMHTHAIN
(see further)

PÁDRAIG
bapt. 17.12.1865

RA
t.
.1852

TOMÁS Ó CRIOMHTHAIN
bapt. 29.04.1855
m. 05.02.1878
d. 07.03.1937
= MÁIRE NÍ CATHÁIN
bapt. 09.02.1859

TOMÁS and MÁIRE
had ten children

others

PÁDRAIG Ó CATHÁIN
bapt. 17.03.1857
m. 10.02.1880
'Rí an Oileáin'
'The Island King'
from c. 1907
Island postman
widower by 1901
(census)
d. 11.06.1929
= EIBHLÍN daughter of Peter/Peadar Ó GAIRBHIA of An Cheathrú Dún Chaoin

NÍ
LLEABHÁIN
.05.1911
.09.1971
family left the
d for the
land in 1942)

MÍCHEÁL

MÁIRE
'MARY PHEATS MHICÍ'
=
MÍCHEÁL Ó GUITHÍN
m. 17.02.1905

CÁIT
'An Princess'
=
SEÁN Ó CATHASA,
Dún Chaoin

'SEÁN AN RÍ'
Island postman
d. 13.06.1934

SEÁN

MÁIRE NÍ GHUITHÍN
'MÁIRE MHAIDHC LÉAN'
b. 19.06.1909

others

BIBLIOGRAPHY

This bibliography includes those books written by the Blasket Islanders and the books written about the Island by the scholar visitors: taken together they make up the Blasket 'library'.

For the general background to the Island and its culture, Robin Flower's book *The Western Island* is the best and most accessible of the works on the subject. For information on archaeology and the early Christian history of the Blaskets, Judith Cuppage's *Corca Dhuibhne – Dingle Peninsula Archaeological Survey* is one of the best surveys of its kind and has the answers to most queries. The *Journal of the Kerry Archaeological and Historical Society* contains a considerable amount of material relating to the Corca Dhuibhne peninsula and to its culture: I have touched on some of that material both here and in the text. Recently a young scholar, Nuala Ní Aimhirgín, wrote a short but very important study of Muiris Ó Súilleabháin, author of *Fiche Blian ag Fás* (*Twenty Years a-Growing*): her book, *Muiris Ó Súilleabháin* (1983) and her research and sources are a useful addition to Blasket scholarship.

Almqvist, B, review of *Allagar na hInise*, *Béaloideas: Journal of Folklore of Ireland Society*, vols 45-7 (1977-9). Contains valuable identification of some of the Islanders in Von Sydow's 1924 photographs.

Barrington, Richard M., 'Report on the flora of the Blasket Islands, County Kerry', *Proceedings of the Royal Irish Academy*, vol 111 (Science), no. 6 (1881)

Barrington, T.J., *Discovering Kerry*, Blackwater, Dublin, 1976

Cuppage, Judith, *Corca Dhuibhne – Dingle Peninsula Archaeological Survey*, Oidhreacht Chorca Dhuibhne, Ballyferriter, 1986

de Brún, Pádraig, 'An tAthair Brasbie', *Journal of the Kerry Archaeological and Historical Society*, no. 2 (1969)

de Brún, Pádraig, 'John Windele and Father John Casey: Windele's visit to Inis Tuaisceart in 1838', *Journal of the Kerry Archaeological and Historical Society*, no. 7 (1974)

de Brún, Pádraig, 'Census of the parish of Ferriter 1835' and 'A Ventry Convert Group 1842', *Journal of the Kerry Archaeological and Historical Society*, no. 13, 1980

Fanning, T., 'Excavation of an early Christian cemetery and settlement at Riask, County Kerry', *Proceedings of the Royal Irish Academy*, vol 81C, no. 3 (1981)

Flower, Robin, *The Western Island*, Oxford University Press, Oxford, 1944

Flower, Robin, *The Irish Tradition*, Oxford University Press, Oxford, 1947

Foley, Patrick, *The Ancient and Present State of the Skelligs, Blasket Island, Donquin and the West of Dingle*, An Cló-chumann Teoranta, Dublin, 1903

Í Chearnaigh, Seán Sheáin, *An tOileán a Tréigeadh*, Sairséal agus Dill, Baile Átha Cliath, 1974

Í Chearnaigh, Seán Sheáin, *Iarbhlaoscadach ina Dheoraí*, Sairséal agus Dill, Baile Átha Cliath, 1978

Irish Coast Pilot (5th edition), Hydrographic Office, Admiralty, London, 1903

Jackson, Kenneth, 'Scéalta ón mBlascaod', *Béaloideas: Journal of the Folklore Society of Ireland*, vol 8, no. 1 (1938)

McGrath, Walter and David Rowlands, 'The Dingle train in the life and lore of Corkaguiny', *Journal of the Kerry Archaeological and Historical Society*, no. 11 (1978)

Marstrander, Carl, *Lidt Af Hvert Fra Irland* (impressions from Ireland), Christiania, Oslo, 1909

Mason, Thomas H., *The Islands of Ireland*, B.T. Batsford, London, 1936

Ní Aimhirgín, Nuala, *Muiris Ó Súilleabháin*, An Sagart, Maynooth, 1983

Ní Ghuithín, Máire, *An tOileán a Bhí*, An Clóchomhar Teoranta, Baile Átha Cliath, 1978

Ní Ghuithín, Máire, *Bean an Oileán*, Coiscéim, Baile Átha Cliath, 1986

Ní Shéaghdha, Nóra, *Thar Bealach Isteach*, Oifig an tSoláthair, Baile Átha Cliath, 1940

Ní Shéaghdha, Nóra, *Peats na Baintrí*, Oifig an tSoláthair, Baile Átha Cliath, 1945

Ní Shúilleabháin, Eibhlís, *Letters from the Great Blasket*, ed. Seán Ó Coileáin, Mercier, Cork, 1978

Ó Cíosáin, Mícheál, *Céad Bliain 1871-1971*, Muintir Phiarais, Baile an Fheirtéaraigh, 1973

Ó Coileáin, Seán, 'Tomás Ó Criomhthain, Brian Ó Ceallaigh agus An Seabhac', *Scríobh 4*, eag. Seán Ó Mórdha (1979)

Ó Conchúir, Donncha, *Corca Dhuibhne*, Clódhanna Teoranta, Baile Átha Cliath, 1973

Ó Conaire, Breandán, 'Ómós do Thomás Ó Criomhthain', *Comhar*, Márta-Lúnasa (1977)

ó Criomhthain, Seán, *Lá dár Saol*, Oifig an tSoláthair, Baile Átha Cliath, 1969

Ó Criomhthain, Seán, 'Tomás Ó Criomhthain mar is cuimhin lena mhac é', *Feasta*, Eanáir (1957)

Ó Criomhthain, Seán, 'Seanchas ón mBlascaod', *Leoithne Aniar*, eag. Pádraig Tyers, Cló Dhuibhne, Baile an Fheirtéaraigh, 1982

Ó Criomhthain, Tomás, *Allagar na hInise*, eag. An Seabhac, C.S. Ó Fallúin i gcomhar le hOifig an tSoláthair, Baile Átha Cliath, 1928

Ó Criomhthain, Tomás, *Allagar na hInise* (2nd edition), eag. Pádraig Ua Maoileoin, Oifig an tSoláthair, Baile Átha Cliath, 1977

Ní Shéaghdha, Nóra, *Peats na Baintrí*, Oifig an tSoláthair, Baile Átha Cliath, 1945

Ó Criomhthain, Tomás, *An tOileánach*, eag. An Seabhac, C.S. Ó Fallúin i gcomhar le hOifig an tSoláthair, Baile Átha Cliath, 1929

Ó Criomhthain, Tomás, *An tOileánach* (2nd edition), eag. Pádraig Ua Maoileoin, Cló Talbot, Baile Átha Cliath, 1973

Ó Criomhthain, Tomás, *An tOileánach* (current edition), Helicon Teoranta, Baile Átha Cliath, 1980

Ó Criomhthain, Tomás, *Dinnsheanchas na mBlascaodaí*, Oifig an tSoláthair, Baile Átha Cliath, 1935

O'Crohan, Tomás, *The Islandman*, trans. Robin Flower, Talbot Press, Dublin and Chatto & Windus, London, 1937; Penguin, Harmondsworth, 1943; Oxford University Press, Oxford, 1951

O'Crohan, Tomás, *Island Cross-Talk*, trans. Tim Enright, Oxford University Press, Oxford, 1986

Ó Danachair, Caoimhín, 'An Rí (the King): an example of traditional social organisation', *Journal of the Royal Society of Antiquaries of Ireland*, vol 111 (1981)

Ó Dubhda, Seán, *An Duanaire Duibhneach*, Oifig an tSoláthair, Baile Átha Cliath, 1933

Ó Dubhda, Seán, 'Cogadh na talún i gCorca Dhuibhne', *Leabhrán Duais-iarrachtaí*, An tOireachtas, Baile Átha Cliath, 1944

Ó Duilearga, Séamas, *Seanchas ón Oileán Tiar*, Comhlucht Oideachais na Éireann Teoranta agus An Cumann le Béaloideas Éireann, Baile Átha Cliath, 1956. (This book is a collection of Island stories and poetry collected by Robin Flower from Tomás Ó Criomhthain. The late Professor Séamas Ó Duilearga edited the material for publication and provided a series of informative notes on people and places in the Blasket Island cluster which is an important source of reference for those interested in the details of the Blasket culture.)

Ó Faoláin, Seán, *An Irish Journey*, Readers' Union with Longmans Green, London, 1941. (Seán Ó Faoláin, who visited the Island, met Tomás Ó Criomhthain and other Islanders and was not impressed: his view is a useful antidote to the enthusiasm of others for the Island and its culture.)

Ó Fiannachta, Pádraig, 'Aibhleoga léinn agus litríochta — V: an chaibidil dheireannach den Oileánach', *An Sagart*, Samhradh (1970)

Ó Fiannachta, Pádraig, 'Allagar na hInise', *Léas ar ár Litríocht*, An Sagart, Má Nuad, 1974

Ó Gaoithín, Mícheál, *Is Trua ná Fanann an Óige*, Oifig an tSoláthair, Baile Átha Cliath, 1953

Ó Gaoithín, Mícheál, *Coinnle Corra*, An Clóchomhar Teoranta, Baile Átha Cliath, 1968

Ó Gaoithín, Mícheál, *Beatha Pheig Sayers*, Foilseacháin Náisiúnta Teoranta, Baile Átha Cliath, 1970

O'Guiheen, Mícheál, *A Pity Youth does not Last*, trans. Tim Enright, Oxford University Press, Oxford, 1982. (This translation also contains a selection of Mícheál Ó Gaoithín's poetry from *Coinnle Corra*.)

Ó Háinle, Cathal, 'Tomás Ó Criomhthain agus "Caisleán Í Néill"', *Irisleabhar Mhá Nuad*, An Sagart, Má Nuad, 1985

Ó hÓgáin, Éamonn, *Díolaim Focal (A) ó Chorca Dhuibhne*, Acadamh Ríoga na hÉireann, Baile Átha Cliath, 1984. (This word collection from the west Kerry area includes many examples from the speech of the former Islanders.)

Ó Lúing, Seán, 'Robin Flower, oileánach agus máistir léinn', *Journal of the Kerry Archaeological and Historical Society*, no. 10 (1977)

Ó Lúing, Seán, 'Seoirse Mac Tomáis — George Derwent Thomson', *Journal of the Kerry Archaeological and Historical Society*, no. 13 (1980)

Ó Lúing, Seán, 'Carl Marstrander (1883-1965)', *Journal of the Cork Historical and Archaeological Society*, vol LXXXIX, no. 248 (1984)

Ó Madagáin, Breandán, 'Functions of Irish song in the nineteenth century', *Béaloideas: Journal of the Folklore of Ireland Society*, vol. 53 (1985)

Ó Súilleabháin, Muiris, *Fiche Blian ag Fás*, Clólucht an Talbóidigh, Baile Átha Cliath, 1933

Ó Súilleabháin, Muiris, *Fiche Blian ag Fás* (2nd edition), An Sagart, Má Nuad, 1976

Ó Súilleabháin, Muiris, *Fiche Blian ag Fás* (3rd edition), An Sagart, Má Nuad, 1981

O'Sullivan, Maurice, *Twenty Years a-Growing*, trans. Moya Llewelyn Davies and George Thomson, Chatto & Windus, London, 1933; Penguin, Harmondsworth, 1938; Oxford University Press, Oxford, 1953

O'Sullivan, Thomas, F., *Romantic Hidden Kerry*, The Kerryman, Tralee, 1931

Sayers, Peig, *Peig*, eag. Máire Ní Chinnéide, Clólucht an Talbóidigh Teoranta, Baile Átha Cliath, 1936

Sayers, Peig, *Machtnamh Seana-Mhná*, eag. Máire Ní Chinnéide, Oifig an tSoláthair, Baile Átha Cliath, 1939

Sayers, Peig, *Machnamh Seanmhná* (2nd edition), eag. Pádraig Ua Maoileoin, Oifig an tSoláthair, Baile Átha Cliath, 1980

Sayers, Peig, *Peig: the autobiography of Peig Sayers of the Great Blasket Island*, trans. Bryan MacMahon, Talbot Press, Dublin, 1974

Sayers, Peig, *An Old Woman's Reflections*, trans. Séamus Ennis, Oxford University Press, Oxford, 1962

An Seabhac (Pádraig Ó Siochfhradha), *Triocha-Céad Chorca Dhuibhne*, Comhlucht Oideachais na hÉireann Teoranta do Cumann le Béaloideas Éireann, Baile Átha Cliath, 1939. (An indispensable source book to unravel the placenames of the barony of Corca Dhuibhne. We await Breandán Ó Ciobháin's volume on Corca Dhuibhne and the Blaskets in his monumental series on the placenames of Kerry, *Toponomia Hiberniae*, An Foras Duibhnearch, Dublin, 1978-.)

An Seabhac (Pádraig Ó Siochfhradha), 'Tomás Ó Criomhthain, Iascaire agus Údar', *Boneventura*, Samhradh (1937)

Sjoestedt-Jonval, Marie-Louise, *Phonétique d'un parler irlandais de Kerry*, Leroux, Paris, 1931

Sjoestedt-Jonval, Marie-Louise, *Description d'un parler irlandais de Kerry*, Champion, Paris, 1938

Sjoestedt-Jonval, Marie-Louise, *Dieux et héros des Celtes*, Presses Universitaires, Paris, 1940

Sjoestedt-Jonval, Marie-Louise, *Gods and Heroes of the Celts*, trans. Myles Dillon, 2nd edition, Turtle Island Foundation, Berkeley, California, 1982 (For her studies on the Irish language dialect of west Kerry, Marie Sjoestedt visited Dún Chaoin and the Blasket Islands in the years 1925 to 1929 and in 1933, and became a good friend of the Islanders. Known as 'Máire Fhrancach', she worked with Peig Sayers, Tomás Ó Criomhthain, Mícheál Ó Gaoithín (An File) and Máire Ní Ghuithín.)

Stagles, Joan and Ray Stagles, *The Blasket Islands*, The O'Brien Press, Dublin, 1980

Stagles, Joan, 'Nineteenth-century settlements in the lesser Blasket Islands', *Journal of the Kerry Archaeological and Historical Society*, no. 8 (1975)

Stagles, Ray, *Day Visitors Guide to the Great Blasket Island*, The O'Brien Press, Dublin, 1982

Stephens, Lilo, *My Wallet of Photographs: the photographs of J.M. Synge*, Dolmen Editions, Dublin, 1971. (There are some errors of identification in My Wallet of Photographs of Blasket Islanders: these are correctly identified in this book.)

Stewart, James, 'An tOileánach — more or less', *Zeitschrift fr Celtische Philologie*, Band 35 (1976)

Synge, John Millington, *In Wicklow and West Kerry*, Maunsel and Company, Dublin, 1912

Synge, John Millington, *Poems and Translations*, Cuala Press, Dublin, 1909

Thomas, Dylan, *A Film Script of 'Twenty Years a-Growing'*, from the story by Maurice O'Sullivan, J.M. Dent & Sons Limited, London, 1964

Thomson, George (Seoirse Mac Tomáis), *An Blascaod Mar a Bhí*, An Sagart, Má Nuad, 1977

Thomson, George, *The Blasket That Was: the story of a deserted village*, An Sagart, Maynooth, 1982

Thomson, George, *The Prehistoric Aegean*, Lawrence & Wishart, London, 1949

Thomson, George, *Aeschylus and Athens*, Lawrence & Wishart, London, 1941

Thomson, George, *Greek Lyric Metre*, Cambridge University Press, Cambridge, 1929

Thomson, George, *Breith báis ar eagnaí*, Oifig an tSoláthair, Baile Átha Cliath, 1929

(For an extensive bibliography of Thomson's work and his publications in Irish, see Seán Ó Lúing, *Journal of the Kerry Archaeological and Historical Society*, no. 13 (1980).)

Ua Duinnín, Pádraig, *Dánta Phiarais Feiritéir*, Oifig an tSoláthair, Baile Átha Cliath, 1934

Ua Maoileoin, Pádraig, *Na hAird ó Thuaidh*, Sairséal agus Dill, Baile Átha Cliath, 1960

Ua Maoileoin, Pádraig, *Bríde Bhán*, Sairséal agus Dill, Baile Átha Cliath, 1968

Ua Maoileoin, Pádraig, *Ó Thuaidh!*, Sairséal-Ó Marcaigh Teoranta, Baile Átha Cliath, 1983

Wignall, Sydney, *In Search of Spanish Treasure: a diver's story*, David & Charles, Newton Abbot, 1982

Wilson, T.G., *The Irish Lighthouse Service*, Allen Figgis, Dublin, 1968

Index

(p) = photograph

Abbey Theatre, The, 135
Achill Missionary Settlement, Co Mayo, 41
agriculture, 46-50
    booleying, 31
    movement of stock, 31
    potato-ridges, 80(p)
Allagar na hInise (Ó Criomhthain), 48, 96, 139, 142-6, 162
Anglo-Normans, 44
archaeology, 28

Baile an Ghoilín, Co Kerry, 67
Baile an Mhúraig, Co Kerry, 50
Baile an Oileáin, Great Blasket, 16(p), 18(p), 19(p), 21(p), 33, 37-9, 65(p), 84(p); see also Barr an Bhaile, Bun an Bhaile
Baile an Teampaill, Co Kerry, 122
Baile na nGall, Co Kerry, 50, 123
Baile Uachtarach, Co Kerry, 43
Baile Viocáire, Dún Chaoin, Co Kerry, 110(p), 111(p), 112(p), 156, 161
Ballyferriter, Co Kerry, 54, 56, 127, 130, 156
Barra an Dá Ghleann, Great Blasket, 60
Barr an Bhaile, Great Blasket, 37, 38, 46, 78(p), 84(p)
Barr a' Niúinigh, Great Blasket, 93(p)
Barrington, Richard, 41, 45-6
(An) Bealach Mór, 17(p), 31, 33, 35-6
Bealach Oileáin na nOg, 32
Bean an Oileáin (Ní Ghuithín), 162
Beiginis, 27, 32-3, 35, 91(p)
    population, 34
    sheep on, 49-50
'Bláithín' see Flower, Robin
(An)Blascaod Mar a Bhí, (The Blasket that Was) (Thomson), 155
(An) Blascaod Mór see Great Blasket, The
Blasket Islands
    archaeology, 28
    geology of, 27
    names of, 27
    population of, 34-5
Blasket sound see Bealach Mór
boat-building, 50-51, 60(p)
Bóithrín na Maiubh, Great Blasket, 19(p)
booleying, 31
Bríde Bhán (Ua Maoileoin), 162
Bun an Bhaile, Great Blasket, 17(p), 34, 37, 38, 46, 84(p), 91(p), 97(p), 104(p)
    Ó Criomhthain house, 131
    Sayers house, 157

Cahirciveen, Co Kerry, 132
Cáit Jim (friend of Peig Sayers), 156, 157
Caladh an Oileáin, Great Blasket, 33, 34, 52, 65(p), 83(p), 84(p), 109(p)
    building of, 34, 99(p), 137, 149
Caoineadh na bPúcaí, 18, 29, 37, 70
Carraig, Co Kerry, 123
Carraig an Lóchair, Great Blasket, 28, 139
Casey, Fr John, 30, 34
castles, 37, 43
Cathedral Rocks, Inis na Bró, 24, 31
Ceann an Dúna, Dun Chaoin, Co Kerry, 17(p), 35
Ceann Dubh, Great Blasket, 31
Ceann Sibéal, Co Kerry, 91(p)
Céitinn, Seathrún, 50
Chambers, George, 72, 117, 162
Clare, County, 50
Cnoc an Bhróigín, Dingle, Co Kerry, 156
Cnocán na gCaorach, Killarney, Co Kerry, 43
Coinnle Corra (Ó Gaoithín), 161
Conchúir, Eoghan Bán, 42
Conchur family, 40
Congested Districts Board, The, 34, 46, 137, 149, 157
Connor, Tom, 123(p)
Corca Dhuibhne, Co Kerry, 27, 43
    gaeltacht, 27
    Ó Siochfhradha papers, 144
    ringforts, 28
    religious controversy, 41
Corcoran, John, 99 (p)
Cork, Earl of, 32, 41, 46
crops, 47
Cruach Mhártain, Co Kerry, 16(p)
Cuan an Chaoil, Co Kerry, 28, 43
Cuas Fada, Beiginis, 32
Cuas na Nae, Co Kerry, 50
currachs see naomhóga

Daideo Eoghan see Ó Suilleabháin, Eoghan
(An) Dáil, Great Blasket, 34, 48
Dálach na hInise, see Ó Dála, Tomás
Davies, Moya Llewelyn, 151, 153
Desmond, Earl of, 36, 43, 127
    landlord of Blaskets, 44-5
Dictionary of the Irish Language (Marstrander), 136
Dingle, Co Kerry, 46, 50, 132, 148, 149
Dingle and Ventry Missionary Society, 18
Dinnsheancha na mBlascaodaí (Ó Criomhthain), 47, 147

Doire Fhatharta, Carraroe, Co Galway, 153
Dublin Opinion, 161
(An) Dún, Great Blasket, 28, 139
Dún an Óir, Co Kerry, 36
Dún Chaoin, Co Kerry, 14(p), 61, 62(p), 69(p), 123
    burials, 19, 56, 131
    cattle to, 85
    education in, 39
    harbour, 33, 87(p)
    mass-going, 81(p)
    wool, 64
Dún Mór, Dún Chaoin, Co Kerry, 33, 35
Du Noyer, George, 31

economy
    agriculture, 46-50
    fishing, 50-53
education, 39-40
Education, Department of, 39
Egan, Fr, 46
Elizabeth I, Queen of England, 36
Ellmann, Richard, 134-5
emigration, 78(p), 150
    and language, 40
English
    teaching of, 39-40, 66
Ennis, Seamus, 160
entertainment 79(p)
Eoghan Bán (weaver), 18(p)
Eoghan Sheáin Eoghain, 70(p)
evacuation, 14, 37, 119, 124(p)

family relationships, 53-6
Feiritéar, Piaras, 43-4, 56
Féiritéaraigh family, 37, 43-4
Feothanach, Co Kerry, 123
(An) Fhaill Mhór, Dún Chaoin, Co Kerry, 33
Fiche Blian ag Fás (Ó Súilleabháin), 54, 78, 148-53
"Fiche Blian faoi Bhláth" (Ó Súilleabháin), 153
field system, 46-7
fishing, 50-53, 67(p), 130-31
FitzGerald, Maurice, 44
Flint, Peatsaí, see Ó Guithín, Pádraig
Flower, Patrick, 106(p)
Flower, Robin, 27, 38, 40, 60(p), 92, 104-7(p), 144, 147, 148
    and Ó Criomhthain, 94(p), 99(p), 103, 136-9, 153
    and Peig Sayers, 158
Foras Feasa ar Éirinn (Céitinn), 50
Forster, E. M., 151

Gabha, Roibeárd, 39
Gaelic League, The, 133

Garda Síochána, 150
Gayer, Rev. Charles, 41
geology, 27
Gillet, Louis, 134
Glouster, James, 123(p)
Goodman, Rev. James, 123
Goodwyn family, 50
Gorky, Maxim, 140, 145
(An) Gort Bán, Great Blasket, 41
graveyards, 64
Great Blasket, The, 13(p), 14(p), 17(p), 27, 33-5, 69(p)
    An Leaca Dhúch, 32
    harbour see Caladh an Oileáin
    martello tower, 36, 48, 60(p)
    Ó Dála family, 70
    placenames, 52-3
    promontory fort, 28, 139
    schools, 18(p), 40-42, 66(p)
    strand see An Trá Bhán
    Trá Ghearraí, 32
    village see Baile an Oileáin, 33
    wells, 48
Gregory, Lady, 135
Grey, Lord, 36
(An) Gúm, 151

Hartney family, 50
Haughey, Charles J., 28
Heaney, Seamus, 29
Horniman, Miss, 135
hurling, 20
Hussey, Miss Clara, 32

Iarbhlascaodach in a Dheoraí (I Chearnaigh), 162
Inis Gé, Co Mayo, 38
Inis Icíleáin, 13(p), 27, 28-9, 31, 51, 52, 149
    fairy music, 18, 29, 37
    landing place, 68(p)
    monastic site, 28
    name of, 28-9
    Ó Criomhthain on, 128-30
    population, 34, 38
    Tig na hInise, 69(p), 70(p)
Inismurray, Co Sligo, 38
Inis na Bró, 13(p), 24(p), 27, 30, 31, 51
Inis Tuaisceart, 13(p), 22(p), 27, 30-31
    landing on, 49
    population, 34
Irish Folklore, Department of UCD, 73
Irish Folklore Commission, 143
Irish language
    study of, 81
    teaching medium, 151
    writing in, 135-7, 144-7

Irish Texts Society, 142
Irish Tradition, The (Flower), 139
Iron Age, 28
Islandman, the, see Ó Criomhthain, Tomás and An t-Oileánach
Is Trua ná Fanann an Óige (Ó Guithín), 161

Jackson, Kenneth, 81(p), 92, 139
    and Peig Sayers, 158
Jordan, James, 41, 123(p)
Joyce, James, 134-5

King of the Island see Ó Catháin, Padraig

Lá dár Saol (S.Ó. Criomhthain), 54, 161-2
landlords, 43-6
(An) Leaca Dhúch, Great Blasket, 32
Leac na Muice, Inis Tuaisceart, 49
Letters from the Great Blasket (Ní Shúilleabháin), 54, 72, 117, 162
lighthouse, 32
literacy, 40-42
(An) Liuir, Co Kerry, 35
lobster fishing, 67(p), 74(p)
'Lochlannach, An' see Marstrander, Carl
Log na bhFiolar, Inis Icíleáin, 69(p), 70(p), 128
Loti, Pierre, 140, 145

Macalister, Professor, R.A.S., 28
McGrath, Walter, 124
Machtnamh Seana-Mhná (Sayers), 160
MacLeod, Caitriona, 112(p)
McMahon, Bryan, 160
MacNeill, Eoin, 136, 143
Mám Clasach, Dingle, Co Kerry, 13
marriages, 53-6
Marstrander, Carl, 92, 135-7, 144
    letter from, 101(p)
    and Ó Criomhthain, 102
    sketches, 88(p)
Marxism and Poetry (Thomson), 154
mass-going, 81(p)
mesolithic period, 28
Mhac an tSaoi, Máire, 44
Mhéine, Séamas, 70(p)
muintir Cheaist see Ó Catháin family
Muiríoch, Ballyferriter, Co Kerry, 119
Mulready, William, 123
Na hÁird Ó Thuaidh (Ua Maoileoin), 162

naomhóga, 33, 34, 35, 46, 59(p), 83(p), 84(p), 86(p), 93(p)
  building of, 60(p)
  crewing of, 55
  description, 50-1
  and evacuation, 124(p)
  fishing, 130
  lobster fishing, 67(p)
  post, 61(p)
  and stock movement, 48-9, 58(p), 85(p)
neolithic period, 28, 91(p)
Ní: note that feminine names (eg Ní Catháin, Ní Shúilleabháin) are entered under the masculine spelling (eg Ó Catháin, Ó Súilleabháin)
Nicholls, Eveleen, 21, 131

O'Brien, Dan, 124
Ó Brosnacháin, Peig (Ní), 156
Ó Catháin, Bríd, 18(p)
Ó Catháin, Cáit (Ní) (An Princess), 121(p), 122(p), 134
Ó Catháin, Cáit (Ní), 153
Ó Catháin, Gearóid, 37
Ó Catháin, Máire (Ní), 130
Ó Catháin, Mairéad (Ní) (Peig Bhofair), 75(p), 77(p), 85(p)
Ó Catháin, Máire (Ní) (Mary Pheats Mhicí), 121(p), 122(p), 133-4
Ó Catháin, Máire Mháire Eoghain, 90(p)
Ó Catháin, Mártan, 129
Ó Catháin, Maurice Muiris, 38, 121(p)
Ó Catháin, Mícheál (Mhicí Bofar), 89(p), 121(p)
Ó Catháin, Neilí (Ní), 121(p)
Ó Catháin, Pádraig (An Rí), 38-9, 39, 99, 120(p), 121(p), 134
  and Flower, 40
  and Marstrander, 135
  Synge in house, 133-4
Ó Catháin, Peig, 22, 30-31, 90(p)
Ó Catháin, Seán an Rí, 39, 61(p), 81(p), 85(p), 92(p)
Ó Catháin, Seán Cheaist, 18(p), 29, 37
Ó Catháin, Seán Faoillí, 38, 51-2
Ó Catháin, Siobhán (Ní) (June Bhofair), 90(p)
Ó Catháin, Tomás, 22, 30-1
Ó Catháin family (muintir Cheaist), 37
Ó Cathasa, Seán, 122
Ó Ceallaigh, Brian, 94, 139-42, 144-6, 159, 162
Ó Ceallaigh, Tadhg, 102
Ó Ceallaigh, Cáit (Ní) (Kate Filí), 76(p)
Ó Cearna, Eibhlín Pheats Taim (Ní), 75(p), 77(p)
Ó Cearna, Maidhc (Sheáisí) 74(p)

Ó Cearna, Máire (Ní) (Mary Filí), 76(p)
Ó Cearna, Máire Pheats Taim (Ní), 75(p), 77(p)
Ó Cearna, Máire (Ní) (Sheáisí), 77(p)
Ó Cearna, Seán (Filí), 74(p)
Ó Cearna, Seán Pheats Taim, 49-50, 75(p)
Ó Cearna, Siobhán (Ní), 76(p)
Ó Cearna, Siobhán (Ní) (Hanna Pheats Taim), 77(p)
Ó Cearna, Tom, 91(p)
Ó Cearna, Tomás Pheats Taim, 75(p)
Ó Cearna family, 40
Ó Cearnaigh, Seán Sheáin I, 162
Ó Cearúl, Risteárd, 33
Ó Cinnéide (Ní), Gobnait, 77
Ó Cinnéide, Máire (Ní), 159
Ó Cinnéide, Professor Seán, 28-9
Ó Cinnéide, Tomás (Cinnéidí an píobaire), 123(p)
Ó Conchúir, Cáit (Ní), 127
Ó Connalláin, Léan (Ní), 159
O'Connell, Daniel, 32
Ó Criomhthain, Cáit (Ní) (daughter Tomás), 131
Ó Criomhthain, Cáit (Ní) (sister Tomás), 148
Ó Criomhthain, Conchúr, 127
Ó Criomhthain, Dónal, 127, 131
Ó Criomhthain, Eibhlín (Ní), 131
Ó Criomhthain, Máire (Ní), 54, 128, 129-30
Ó Criomhthain, Muiris, 131-2, 149
Ó Criomhthain, Neill (Ní), 132
Ó Criomhthain, Niamh (Ní), 71(p)
Ó Criomhthain, Nóra (Ní), 128
Ó Criomhthain, Pádraig, 131
Ó Criomhthain, Pádraig (Snr), 131
Ó Criomhthain, Seán, 54, 71(p), 72, 118(p), 119(p), 131-2, 149, 161-2
Ó Criomhthain, Tomás, 21, 88(p), 94-100(p), 119, 131, 162.
  see also Allagar na hInise; An tOileánach
  and An Seabhac, 116
  describes Inis Tuaisceart, 30
  family of, 54, 130-2
  family relationships, 54-5
  and Flower, 40
  house of, 38, 46, 71(p)
  influences on, 127-47
  and Jordan, 41
  and Marstrander, 102(p)
  and Ó Ceallaigh, 159
  and Peig Sayers, 158
  on Piaras Feiritéar, 44
  postcard from, 103(p)
  quoted on Island life, 19, 20, 32, 39, 45, 46, 48
  relations of, 54
  schooldays, 39
Ó Dála, Pádraig, 70(p)

Ó Dála, Tomás (Tom na hInise), 29, 69(p), 70(p), 128
Ó Dála family, 68(p), 128-9
  house, 69(p)
Ó Dálaigh, Cáit (Ní), 33
Ó Donncha, Neans (Ní), 39
Ó Duilearga, Professor Séamas, 143
Ó Duinnshlé, Séamus, 121(p)
Ó Duinnshlé, Seán, 140-2, 162
Ó Duinnshlé, Siobhán (Ní), 72(p)
Ó Duinnshlé, Tomás, 38, 121(p)
Ó Duinnshlé, Tomás Mháire Bhell Eoghain I, 16(p)
Ó Duinnshlé family, 17(p), 38
Ó Faoláin, Seán, 27
Ó Gaoithín, Mícheál (Maidhc File), 54, 110, 114-16(p), 149, 157-8, 159, 161
Ó Gearailt, Máire (Ní), 40
Ó Guithín, Cáit (Ní), 148, 157
Ó Guithín, Eibhlín (Neilí) (Ní), 157-8
Ó Guithín, Lís (Ní), 149
Ó Guithín, Máire (Ní) (Máire Mhaidhc Léan), 77(p), 104(p), 162
Ó Guithín, Máire (Ní) (Mary Pheats Mhicí), 39, 40, 81(p), 104(p)
  house of, 92p
Ó Guithín, Mícheál, 112(p), 121(p)
Ó Guithín, Mícheál (Maidhc Ghobnait), 77(p)
Ó Guithín, Muiris, 157
Ó Guithín, Muiris Mhaidhc Léan, 77(p)
Ó Guithín, Pádraig, 157, 159
Ó Guithín, Pádraig (Peatsaí Flint), 53-4, 157
Ó Guithín, Seana Mhicí, 53
Ó Guithín, Seán Mhaidhc Léan, 38
Ó Guithín, Tomás, 157, 159-60
Ó Guithín family, 39
Oíbleán, St, 28-9
Oileán Eile — Another Island (film), 12, 155
Oileán na nÓg, 27, 33
(An) Oileán Tiar see Great Blasket, The
Ó Laoghaire, Fr Peadar, 135, 145
Ó Mainín, Cait (Ní), 149
Ó Muircheartaigh, Seán (Seán a' Scraiste) 132
Ó Muicheartaigh, Tomás, 41
Ó Muirgheasáin, Maol Domhnaigh, 43
Ó Ríordáin, Seán, 116(p)
Ó Scannláin, Máire (Ní), 38, 161
Ó Sé, Cáit (Ní), 127
Ó Sé, Diarmaid, 128, 129
Ó Sé, Nessa (Ní) (Bean Í Dheoráin), 112(p)
Ó Sé, Nóra (Ní), 70(p)
Ó Séaghdha, Nóra (Ní), 66(p)
Ó Siochfhradha, Pádraig (An Seabhac), 140, 143-4, 158

Ó Súilleabháin, Eibhlín (Neilí Sheáin Lís), 94(p), 159
Ó Súilleabháin, Eibhlís (Lís), 54, 70-72(p), 80, 117(p), 118(p), 119, 162
Ó Súilleabháin, Eilín (Ní), 149
Ó Súilleabháin, Eoghan (Daideo Eoghan), 37, 108(p), 148, 149-50, 152, 155
Ó Súilleabháin, Eoin, 153
Ó Súilleabháin, Maidhc, 72(p)
Ó Súilleabháin, Máire (Ní), 53, 149
Ó Súilleabháin, Máire (2), 72(p)
Ó Súilleabháin, Máirín, 153
Ó Súilleabháin, Mícheal, 123
Ó Súilleabháin, Muiris, 37, 63, 87, 94, 108-10(p), 148-55, 158, 161, 162
  see also Fiche Blian ag Fás
Ó Súilleabháin, Pádraig, 72(p)
Ó Súilleabháin, Seáinín Mhicí, 72(p)
Ó Súilleabháin, Seán Lís, 148, 149
Ó Súilleabháin, Seán Mhicí, 72(p)
Ó Súilleabháin, Siobhán (née Ní Dhuinnshlé), 80(p)
Ó Súilleabháin families, 37
Ó Thuaidh! (Ua Maoileoin), 162
(An) tOileán a Bhí (Ní Ghuithín), 162
(An) tOileánach (Ó Criomhthain), 96, 127, 139, 143-4, 146, 150, 162
  translation of 153
(An tOileán a Tréigeadh (I Cearnaigh), 162

Paróiste Chill Chúain, Great Blasket, 66
Pearse, Patrick, 21, 131, 145
Peig (Sayers), 158
Playboy of the Western World (Synge), 133, 134
Poll na Stiúrach, Tiaracht, 23(p)
  population, 34-5
  postman, 39, 61(p)
  potato-picking, 80(p)
Prehistoric Aegean, The (Thomson), 154
Prométheus faoi Chuibhreach (Thomson), 154
promontory fort, 28, 31, 36, 139
Protestant mission, 18, 40-1, 42, 123(p)

Raidió na Gaeltachta, 40
Raleigh, Sir Walter, 36
rent collection, 45-6
Rí an Oileáin see Ó Catháin, Padraig
ringforts, 28
Rinn an Chaisleáin, Great Blasket, 37, 38, 43, 64(p)
Rinn Chaol, Inis Icíleáin, 68(p)
Ross Castle, Co Kerry, 43
  rundale system, 47
  sand-gathering, 63(p)

Savage, Lís, 77(p)
Savage, Sissy, 77(p)
Savage, Thomas, 149
Savage, Treasa, 77(p)
Sayers, Eibhlín (Neilí Pheig), 76(p), 113(p)
Sayers, Máire, 156
Sayers, Pádraig, 156, 157
Sayers, Peig, 33, 46, 113-14(p), 116(p), 156-61, 162
  children, 149
  marriage of, 53-4
Sayers, Seán, 156
Sayers, Tomás, 156
Scairt Phiaras, Great Blasket, 44
Scéalta ón mBlascaod (Jackson), 158
schools, 18, 40-42, 66(p)
Scoil an Bhlascaoid, Great Blasket, 39-40, 66(p)
Scoil an tSúip, Great Blasket, 18(p), 40-2
(An) Scológ, near Great Blasket, 33, 35
Seabhac, An see Ó Siochfhradha, Pádraig
seals, 15(p)
  hunting of, 24, 31, 53
Seanchas ón Oileán Tiar (Flower), 139, 147
seaweed-gathering, 21, 79(p)
Shanachie, The, 133
sheep-shearing, 64(p)
Simonds-Gooding, Maria, 161
Sliabh an Iolair, Dún Chaoin, Co Kerry, 27
Sliabh Bharra an Dá Ghleann, Great Blasket, 48, 60
(An) Slinneán Bán, Great Blasket, 46, 89(p), 90(p), 110(p), 137, 149, 157
Smerwick Harbour, Co Kerry 36
Spanish Armada, 17, 35, 53
Spenser, Edmund, 36
stock, 47-9
  transport of, 48-9, 58(p), 85(p)
Streeter, Ida Mary, 105(p), 138
Stromboli, HMS, 35
Sullivan, Dan, 123(p)
Sullivan, John, 41, 123(p)
Synge, John Millington, 92, 162
  photographs, 120-2
  visits, 132-5

Teampall Bréanainn, Inis Tuaisceart, 30
Thomas, Dylan, 153
Thomson, George, 109(p), 139, 148, 150-5, 162
Tiaracht, 13(p), 27, 31, 32, 49
  lighthouse, 23(p), 32
Tig na Dála, 38
Tobar an Phoncáin, Great Blasket, 48
Tomás Eoghain Bháin, 151
Tom na hInise see Ó Dála, Tomás
Tory Island, Co Donegal, 38

Trá a'Loinnithe, Beiginis, 32
(An) Trá Bhán, Great Blasket 15(p),
    20(p), 32-4, 62(p), 83(p), 106(p),
        131
    sand-gathering, 63(p)
(An) Trá Ghearraí, Great Blasket,
    32, 46, 64
Tralee Castle, Co Kerry, 43
turf-cutting, 47-8, 60(p), 83(p)
Tusnú na Feallsúnachta (Thomson),
    154
*Twenty Years a-Growing see Fiche Blian
    ag Fás*

Ua Maoileoin, Padraig, 144, 162
Uíbh Ráthach, Co Kerry, 127

Ventry, Co Kerry, 54, 123, 151, 156
Ventry, Lord, 41
Von Sydow, Carl, 143
    photographs, 73, 82, 89(p), 113

wells, 48
Western Island, The (Flower), 105, 138
wildlife, 15(p), 24, 30-1, 32, 53
Windele, John, 22, 30
wool, 49-50, 64(p)

Yeats, W.B., 134